ENERGY AND THE CITY

Career Advice from Houston's Energy Executives

Joan Eischen

Misturafina Publishing
2011

Cataloging-in-Publication Data

Eischen, Joan
Energy and the City

I. Energy Industry — Women — Houston
II. Female Professionals — Energy Industry
III. Employment Opportunities — Women — Energy Industry
IV. Houston, TX — Business

TA157 E676 2011   338.76655Ei

Library of Congress Number: 2011917868
ISBN 978-0615540368

Dedication and Acknowledgements

I wasn't certain how to write a dedication; this is my first book. I read that a dedication can be the greatest expression of love one can perform. If that is true, then my first dedication is to my husband Maarten van Hasselt. This book consumed every weekend for over one year and he endured the process; he was encouraging and patient with my emotional swings of a new writer. These women's names were a part of our conversations. He knows them as well as I do.

The women I interviewed inspired me and encouraged me to write *"Energy and the City."* They shared their stories and advice on becoming role models and leaders in the energy industry. I carried their voices in my head and put their words to practice in my own challenges at work. I know they will inspire you too.

To all my friends and advisors who provided the necessary feedback to make this a great book. I am certain I will miss some of the names, but here are a few: Katie and Ally Mehnert and her focus group of young women 28-34 years old. Janet Roth, Monica Brashear, Jana Grauberger, Ann Banks, Rosamond Quay and Ellen Heemer. I can't forget Chris and Laura Schilling because they introduced me to Women's Energy Network and that is where my book started.

Many thanks to Valore D women's group in Italy who invited me to speak at their quarterly event in Florence. These executives are striving to snap the stereotype of women in Italy, a country that trails most of Europe with female board representation. Thank you to Monica Poggio, Irene Recchia, Caterina Silvestri, Anna Marchesi and Federica Rofi. Avanti!

My dedication would not be complete if I didn't include my parents, my sister Jane Kondracki and my niece Kristine Krukar. Your phone calls, advice and words of encouragement during the process meant the world to me.

66 The Energy industry has traditionally been a bastion of maleness. The issue should never be whether the best performance comes from a man or a woman--it is that the best performer ought to be advanced--and if that happens to be a woman, ingrained biases should not come to bear in terms of making advancement decisions. We need strong, capable women to join us. 99
—Marcela Donadio, Americas Oil & Gas Sector Leader, Ernst & Young, Houston

Table of Contents

66 You will make mistakes:
live and learn from them. **99**
—Rebecca McDonald,
CEO for Laurus Energy

Introduction

Your work week could include a meeting in London and a project review in Paris, ending with a conference in Dubai. For some women, a day consists of flying in a helicopter offshore to a rig, wearing a hardhat and steel-tipped boots to analyze rock chippings with the mud loggers. For others, a day at the office might mean managing business in the outskirts of Denver or traveling to North Africa for a twenty-eight-day rotation. Still others are developing new technologies to meet climate change or lobbying the government on new tax regulations. Some prefer working in the countries where their energy company does business, building partnerships with host communities in the Philippines, Kazakhstan, or Brazil. All this is possible with a career in energy.

If you like responsibility and want to be on the forefront of something that impacts the world, a career in energy may be for you. Energy can be defined as fossil fuel, wind, solar, alternative, and green. They are all integrated in our economy, politics, and the environment. Women are leading in roles that were traditionally "for men only," and they are gaining visibility and respect for the roles they are performing. There are few women in senior positions, and the opportunities are abundant.

Women are critical for the future success of the energy industry. Talent scarcity has gained new relevance now that energy is such a hot topic in international politics. In 2008, Shell Oil Company presented three hard truths that apply today: the demand for energy will increase, oil is no longer easy to find, and the stresses on the environment require new technology. These truths require more graduates who hold degrees in STEM careers—Science, Technology, Engineering, and Math—to develop new solutions for the energy industry. Attracting and retaining women with the right skill set is the challenge.

In 2005, I was a managing partner for a global energy magazine. One of my responsibilities was to interview industry leaders. After several months, I realized that I wasn't talking to any women. I reviewed ten years of publications that focused on energy, and I learned that women were not featured as prominent players. Women are still few in the industry.

Could the scarcity of women be due to the lack of interest to study technical careers or do women at some point become discouraged in a male dominant industry? The idea for a book came while I was program director for the Women's Energy Network, a nonprofit association for women working in the energy industry. Through the organization, I was able to meet the women leading in the industry and learn from them the challenges and successes they experienced as women in energy.

Energy and the City profiles thirty-one senior executive women in the energy industry. This book is not an exhaustive study, rather a fireside chat with the women who lead in a male-dominated industry. These corporate pioneers entered the industry at a transitional time, the 1970s and 1980s, when women were hardly present in energy companies. The women I interviewed talked about the changes to both the workplace and home front, which brought for those who followed better work environments and personal choices. The book focuses on the challenges women faced as a minority in a room full of men and how they overcame obstacles.

Some may think that the issue of female career advancement is no longer valid, but the experiences of these women, and my own experience, show that this is not true.

At the beginning of all careers, the pipeline of talent looks the same. As women progress in their careers and personal lives, the pipeline fills with obstacles and filters, making it more of a narrow-ended funnel that keeps many talented females stuck inside. How can energy companies help female professionals through the pipeline to achieve higher career objectives?

The women I interviewed are in the "C-suite" and senior executive level—that is, women working in high-level positions such as CEO, CFO, Partner, President and Executive Vice President. They provide advice for young women who are deciding what they want to study and career path they may want to follow. There are words of wisdom for young hires and mid-level executives who are stuck in the talent pipeline, not understanding why they are not progressing through it. We understand that women are well represented in middle and senior management positions, but in the C-suite, they are outnumbered four to one. Women hold 3 percent of Fortune 500 CEO positions—what's keeping women below the glass ceiling?

In the interviews I conducted, three overarching themes emerged.

Visibility. A leader recognized by Forbes magazine, Janet Clark, executive vice president and CFO for Marathon Oil, leads the discussion on the first major areas: creating your own personal brand and finding your voice in the shift from team player to leader in a male dominated industry.

This book presents advice from executive coaches who work side by side with high potential women and senior executives, helping them navigate the land mines that often derail or stall a successful career.

Sponsors. Lynn Laverty Elsenhans, CEO and President, Sunoco, Inc. and Sunoco Logistics Partners LP, ranked number ten on Forbes "100 Most Powerful Women" list, states "Women need sponsors." High-performing women don't have the sponsorship they need to reach the top. Elsenhans says that women focus too much on mentoring. Chapter four looks at the difference between sponsors and mentors and the importance of networking.

Work/Life. When it comes to women's careers and personal choices, the largest obstacle is work/life decisions. One of Houston's most influential women, Peggy Montana, executive vice president for supply and distribution at Shell Downstream, Inc., gave sound advice for taking on a leadership role and managing children at home. She remembered putting out fires in refineries, her husband traveling and a nanny at home taking care of the children. I present the viewpoints of single women and couples who managed dual careers, most with children. They were all trying to balance life and work.

Their inspiring and frank stories detail their experiences and prove that the glass ceiling can be broken in what is perceived as a male-dominated industry. I understand that not all young women want to be a CEO or CFO or lead engineering projects, so I have included interviews with general counsel, corporate accountants, human resources, and marketing professionals—many of these women learned the technical aspects of the industry on the job.

What you will discover is that the industry is changing due to the resource challenge; both in talent and natural resources. Talent diversity is required to bring different viewpoints to the discussions to develop innovative solutions for the development of alternative and unconventional energy. *"Energy and the City"* will help you navigate some of the challenges of being the only woman in the room and presents some exciting ideas for a fulfilling career.

Houston is the Energy Capital of the World, so my book begins with some important information and statistics that were provided in collaboration with The Greater Houston Partnership. I include a few of the women I interviewed in this chapter. They provide encouraging words to convince young women to study technical degrees that will open up many great opportunities in the energy industry. The women share why they chose Houston and why they are passionate about the industry. They mention options for young graduates who are not technical yet interested in a career in energy. Chapter two will be an introduction to the women with a photo, their title and company where they work. Their biographies can be found in the appendix.

The energy industry is an exciting place to make a career, if you know how to make it happen, but there are many pitfalls and obstacles to overcome that are addressed in chapters three through eight.

We all hope that more women decide to work in the energy industry and see Houston ("The City") as a great place to start a career. Every major energy company is represented in Houston. The women I interviewed either started their careers in Houston or started in a different industry and moved to Houston to work. Some have since moved to new locations with energy companies. During the writing of this book I had one woman leave the industry after twenty three years to pursue a career in her field of expertise that was developed in Houston in energy.

Embarking on a new career can be daunting. If you are uncertain about your place in an organization or industry, you can find yourself wondering, "Is it just me?" While this tendency is not unique to women, the guidance of women who have come before gives you the confidence to move forward in your career from entry level to executive level. *Energy and the City* helps readers to climb the corporate ladder and avoid missteps along the way.

66 Houston is an international city with the kindest, warmest and most charitable people you will ever meet. **99** —The Greater Houston Partnership.

Chapter 1:
Houston, The Energy Capital of the World

In collaboration with Jeff Moseley, president and CEO of the Greater Houston Partnership, who co-wrote this chapter on Houston.

Cities and employers all over the country are competing for educated, young professionals. Where you choose to begin your career may be one of the most important decisions you ever make, because it impacts not only your career but your quality of life.

Search the social media websites, and you will read posts proclaiming Houston as a terrific place to live. The cost of living compared to any other large metropolitan city is moderate. No matter what your interests, Houston can satisfy them with museums, theaters, music, sports, parks, schools, shopping and education. Houstonians agree that it's a comfortable place to live.

Houston is all about energy and not just in a literal sense:
- More than 3,000 energy-related businesses (including more than 500 exploration and production firms)
- More than 150 pipeline transportation establishments
- Hundreds of manufacturers and wholesalers of energy-sector products
- 42 of America's 141 publicly traded oil and gas exploration and production firms
- 9 refineries that produce 2.33 million barrels of crude oil per day
- 50 percent of Texas' total production and 13.5 percent of the total U.S. capacity
- 13 of the nation's 20 largest U.S. interstate oil pipeline companies
- 15 of 20 of the natural gas transmission companies have presence in some capacity
- 60,912 miles (41.5 percent) of U.S. oil pipeline capacity

- 110,295 miles of U.S. gas pipeline (57.3 percent) of U.S. capacity
- Permanent Secretariat of the World Energy Cities Partnership (WECP)[1]

A great place for women

Houston is a great place for young professionals to start a career. The energy industry is a predominantly male one, but that's changing as more and more women realize the incredible opportunities available to them within the industry.

Houston is run by a former energy employee and a woman, Mayor Annise Parker. In this book, she shared her experiences working in the energy industry and how she applies her lessons learned to her role today. Parker showed how the skills learned in the energy sector can be transferred to a high-power position in government. She hopes more women will come to Houston and work in the energy industry.

As the number of women working in the energy sector grows, so do the support organizations, including Young Professionals in Energy, Young Women Energized, WEN, and the Women's Global Leadership Conference.

"I recommend the energy industry to anyone, because the most challenging problems that we have before us are how to keep energy affordable, available, clean, and convenient," Lynn Laverty Elsenhans, CEO and President, Sunoco, Inc. and Sunoco Logistics Partners LP, says. "Once you get into the industry and see what is possible it is an incredibly exciting industry to be a part of and the work is so rewarding that it far outweighs any of the other challenges."

66 I am proud of what I accomplished not just as a woman, but as a leader.99 —Laurie Markoe, President and CEO of Contract Land Staff, LLC.

[1] A collaboration among sixteen energy cities worldwide, providing a platform for information exchange, networking and public relations.

Elsenhans says that in the past, it has been a difficult industry for women. "The industry continues to get better in terms of a comfortable place for women to work. It is a lot different today than it was when I started thirty years ago. There are women at every level from working on the rigs to operations, all the way up to CEO. There are no jobs in this industry today that people would consider strange if it was being led by a woman."

Women are leading in roles that were traditionally "for men only." Susan Cunningham, senior vice president of exploration for Noble Energy, remembered when she started in the industry there were some limitations for women but it changed, allowing her to travel to Africa early on in her career. She did field work in East Africa, where she was responsible for the program and partnership. For six weeks, Cunningham and her team lived in tents in the Riff Valley in Tanzania. The office was a desk outside, and the shower was a tent. As a geologist, her job was to look for the elements that told the story of a good exploration site. Much of the work consisted of walking down the rivers to do the mapping. From time to time, she and a partner had to look over the crops by helicopter. The environment she was working in was remote, with no villages nearby. The locals were subsistence farmers located in and around a preserve, so they had a game hunter that provided them with food. As part of the culture, the Africans built a bonfire after a kill, and donned their masks, and danced to celebrate. They then shared a meal with Cunningham's group. "It was an unbelievable experience you don't get in every industry," says Cunningham. A career in energy can allow for travel, adventure and creating relationships in countries where your company does business.

Samina Farid, chairman of Merrick Systems, sees women progressing and excelling in technical roles. When I interviewed Farid, she had just returned from Malaysia, India, and Saudi Arabia. She was excited because she saw qualified women working in the industry. The Iraqi oil ministry visited her company with seventeen engineers, both men and women. In this Islamic nation, the women traveled outside of their countries and were respected not only in their companies but internationally. That is what the energy industry can offer women: opportunities to be recognized and respected.

Farid started her company over twenty years ago and is one of few women who own a company in the energy industry. She loves the energy industry for the complex challenges. She explains, "It is a global industry, and we face a lot of challenges. You deal with men in the field, you are in an office the next day, and the next day flying to Saudi Arabia. Industry is my passion."

Farid continues, "From day to day, you are dealing with something that impacts the world. It is incredible and important, and I am developing solutions for the industry. There is an amazing diversity of people and cultures that I work with. There are so many aspects and faces to this industry; it is a great industry to be in, and it is continuously evolving."

Many qualified young professionals around the world do not know of the possibilities available through careers in energy, and companies need to do more to attract women to the industry.

Kathleen Eisbrenner, founder and CEO of Next Decade, LLC, says that there is still a gender gap in the energy industry. The ongoing need for skilled, qualified talent appears to be altering the makeup of the traditionally male-dominated industry, slowly but surely. Eisbrenner never anticipated that natural gas would be her career, but she adds, "It has been fantastic, and I love it. It is so important and fundamental to everything we do every day. The overlay of the risk to people and the environment creates the complexity and enhances the importance of the business, so I wish more women would understand the opportunity to get involved in energy."

A great place for education

Education is the cornerstone of the energy industry, and the Houston region is home to more than its share of prestigious universities, including Rice University, the University of Houston, Texas Southern University, the University of St. Thomas, and Houston Baptist University. The University of Houston at Clear Lake, Prairie View A&M University, Sam Houston State

University, Lamar University, and Texas A&M University are all within an hour and a half from downtown Houston.

The Houston region is also home to more than two dozen community college systems and many technical schools and vocational programs, which is a credible and affordable way to get a college degree.

Houston's energy industry offers intern opportunities to hundreds of aspiring professionals, providing excellent entry opportunities for university students and recent graduates.

Suzanne Nimocks is a member of the board of directors for EnCana and Rowan Companies. She is a recently retired director (senior partner) in McKinsey & Company's Houston office and advises women to consider technical studies. Nimocks recommends that young people in general focus their work experience on the operations side of the business within the energy companies, because rising in an organization and gaining visibility is faster with these skills.

She adds, "The industry is a fabulous place for women for a number of reasons. Intellectually it is complex, it is global, and there are many ways that women can contribute. There is an advantage to being in an industry where there are fewer technical women. If you have the capacity to make a difference with a strong and important point of view, you will be heard and remembered, and there is something to be said to being remembered. A woman can create many opportunities for herself."

Meg Gentle, senior vice president and CFO for Cheniere Energy, says that the energy industry is integrated in our economy, politics, and the environment. "Energy is at the core of everybody's life. Everything that we do, especially today, is dependent on energy."

She explains that relations between companies and countries are based on energy. There are opportunities to branch off into economics, politics, or the environment and have an interesting career with great exposure to new cultures, international travel, and the energy debate, which will be strong in the future. "Energy is a very exciting industry to work. It gives you the opportunity to go anywhere you want to go, use a diverse set of skills, and there is a lot of community involvement, too," she adds.

Her company has a program for charitable contributions, and the company gets involved in fun, team-building activities such as biking or running for a cause.

Young people are growing up interconnected in the world, and the culture of the energy industry may appeal to them. Melody Meyer, president of Chevron Asia-Pacific Exploration and Production Company, believed that Houston's energy industry is a great place for young people today. Companies delegate responsibility and authority for major multimillion and billion-dollar projects to talented young people all over the world. With the right training, many exciting opportunities in some exciting places await anyone who wants to work hard.

"It is a very energizing industry and high tech. We are trying to solve the problems by being very creative, so the industry constantly reinvents itself with ideas and hardworking people who have strong values," Meyer says.

A great place for a career

According to The Daily Beast (October 2010), Houston is one of the best cities to start a new career because of its low costs of living, relatively low unemployment rate, and large number of small businesses. Houston also ranks high in the charity-conscious category and is one of the few cities on the list that show positive growth for small businesses.

Houston topped Business Week's list of top cities for recent college graduates. The study ranked thirty of the best U.S. cities based on job openings for new graduates, posted on AfterCollege.com. The rankings were based on highest average annual pay, lowest unemployment rate, and affordable cost of living. Houston ranked number one, followed by Washington, DC, Dallas, Atlanta, and Austin.

"I tell everybody to go into the energy industry because it allows you to be on the forefront of what matters, and Houston is a great place to start an energy career," says Peggy Montana, executive vice president for supply and distribution with Shell Downstream, Inc. "If you want to help solve the world's problems, then this is the place to be. With the increasing demands for resources, coupled with the impact of climate change, we will be involved in the transformation of the energy mix."

The prospect of meeting rising consumption and the challenges to get hydrocarbons out of the ground can be daunting. Climate change is a heated debate that doesn't have any clear resolution, but it creates challenging opportunities for those interested in alternative energy.

Houston has never been a city that rests on its laurels. It takes its moniker "the energy capital of the world" seriously, which means expanding beyond oil and gas to include renewable energy, thereby adding jobs and increasing quality of life. While many graduates are looking for lucrative, competitive careers, they are also passionate about social well-being. They want energy to be profitable and socially responsible.

" Onward! "
—Jeff Moseley,
President and CEO
for the Greater
Houston Partnership.

The focus on "green" energy in Houston has given way to a plethora of new jobs. According to the United States Conference of Mayors, Houston ranked third in the nation for current and potential green jobs. The Houston region is home to more than a dozen major wind energy companies, and almost three dozen companies are active in the solar energy field in the Houston region. According to the National Biodiesel Board, the Gulf Coast region is home to both the nation's largest and third-largest biodiesel plants. Houston is a city of visionaries who care as much about doing what is right as about living well.

Martha Wyrsch, president of Vestas-American Wind Technology, Inc. North America, explains, "There are well-established parts of the energy industry, but there are also brand-new players and brand-new innovative opportunities in renewable energy; - we need it all. We need coal and gas and hydro and nuclear. We clearly need wind and solar and other renewables, so young people looking for a career would find this an industry that has enormous potential that allows them to be innovative." Her advice is, "Choose something that you are passionate about because then you are going to succeed, and you are going to make a difference."

These reports uphold what Houstonians already know: Houston is a great place to start a career for young professionals. An important facet of working in the industry is the opportunity for private philanthropy. The industry does a lot in Houston that goes largely unnoticed – some of the greatest contributors to The United Way, the arts, and museums are energy companies. The companies have contributed both employee time and money toward making Houston a better place to work and live. Some of those values show up in the commitments that the companies make to local communities. Janet Clark of Marathon Oil states that being a good corporate citizen builds relations in the countries where the company does business. She notes that the industry is all about safety and the environment and that each company is trying to "do better and get it right." Her company maintains community programs where it operates, and in Houston, her company is active in a number of organizations including the Susan G. Komen Race for the Cure.

Even with philanthropy, the energy industry's image is not always good. There are a lot of misconceptions in the consumers' minds, so there are great opportunities for improvement, explains Cheryl Chartier vice president for marketing and proposals with Foster Wheeler USA. "We are looking to be more sustainable and to protect the environment. We need everyone to be involved to understand its complexity. I want to be around when the world realizes that we are creating opportunity and that it is a good industry with good people."

A great place to live

Whether you are a high school student interested in the energy sector and considering attending a college in the region, a college graduate considering a move, or an established professional ready to change careers, Houston is a city of opportunity.

Cheryl Chartier came to work in Houston in 1989 because it was a great time for the energy industry. Having earned a mechanical engineering degree, she originally wanted to work in automotive or aeronautics engineering. She had no prior exposure to energy and chose Houston over Detroit because the cost of living was better.

You may be researching a future career in the energy industry or considering a field of study for college. If you want the opportunity to make more money than average and spend less money than average while living in one of the most diverse, dynamic and exciting cities in the United States, give Houston a try.

Unlike the technology industry, in which senior leadership workers are in their twenties or early thirties, the energy industry is getting old. Sue Ortenstone, executive vice president and chief administrative officer of El Paso Corporation says, "What a great opportunity to be in the energy industry right now as a young person, because we need young people to move up in the companies and take charge in the future. You will be in the spot to fuel your career and the economy. The current baby boomer leadership is going to retire, and that will require a changeover."

"We are an energy dependent nation, so whether it is oil or gas or alternative, we have to figure out how we can deliver the best in the safest way. Young people should come to Houston, because the energy industry is not going away. It is shifting and creating new possibilities for an exciting career."

66 Success follows happiness, not the other way around. 99
—Meg Gentle, Senior Vice President and CFO, Cheniere Energy

Chapter 2:
This Isn't Your Daddy's Oil Field Anymore

The energy industry is a rough and tumble industry, but it is no longer just for men. The phrase gender equality has been debated for more than forty years. While a person is biologically male or female, the role of gender is influenced by cultural and social expectations. When women first made their way into management and senior management positions, it was assumed that they had to "act like men" to succeed. The women interviewed for this book prove that leadership is less about gender and more about understanding the demands and complexity of the organization and being able to inspire others to rise to any occasion to complete the task.

❝ If you're prepared to act, you can create significant advantage through change, ❞ says Melody Meyer, President of Chevron Asia-Pacific Exploration and Production Company

Women blazed trails for us in the second half of the twentieth century, and young women entering today's energy workforce face fewer of the overt attitudes and behaviors then in the past. Many of the women I interviewed started their careers in the 1970s and 1980s, when men believed that women should be in the home with the children. Many women commented on the underlying and prevalent uneasiness that they felt.

Most of them did not have female mentors, coaches, and peers who could have made it easier, so they had to trust their instincts and create their own style. They managed behaviors that today we would consider extremely inappropriate such as "Lingerie Friday." The engineering group at one company lunched at a restaurant that included models strolling about in sexy lingerie. To feel part of the group, one female engineer went along. Once she gained confidence in her position, she declined to attend, not to anyone's surprise.

Another woman was chased around her desk by a senior executive. She had to threaten him with her big brother to get him to stop. He was later slapped with a lawsuit by the EEOC, to no one's surprise.

Today, a woman with drive and desire can carve out a meaningful career in the energy industry. Women are no longer the pioneers but innovators in the industry. They learned leadership skills through trial and error, they understood how to be assertive without being abrasive, they found their voices in an environment dominated by men, and they learned to be authentic in their leadership. They showed that there was no cookie-cutter formula approach to authenticity.

Of the thirty-one women I interviewed, twenty-five were married, and most were part of dual-career couples with children. In six families, the husband stepped back in his career, and only two families had stay-at-home fathers (the kids were in high school). Four couples had no children, and I spoke with six single or divorced women, two with children.

Some set their sights on the energy industry; others arrived to it via a serendipitous route. All were college educated but had different majors. Only fourteen had degrees in science, technology, engineering or math (STEM). For the others, their studies ranged from law, accounting, broadcasting, and international relations to economics. Few were from Houston (but they got here as fast as they could). They prove that it is possible to have a career in a male-dominated industry as a single woman or as part of a couple, with or without children, and they inspire young women who are looking for a meaningful career.

You will find their full bios in the appendix. The following pages serve as an introduction to them. The pages contain their professional photos, title and company names to use as a reference as you read about them throughout the book. You will hear their voices in the stories they share and the career advice they provide. I am sure that you will appreciate reading their personal details in the appendix as much as I enjoyed meeting them.

Laura Buss Sayavedra
Vice President & CFO

Spectra Energy Partners, LP

Halina Caravello
Vice President, EH&S

Tyco International

(Formerly employed
with Baker Hughes, Inc.)

Martha Z. Carnes
Partner,
Energy Assurance

PricewaterhouseCoopers LLP

Cheryl Chartier
VP Marketing &
Proposals

Foster Wheeler USA

Janet F. Clark
EVP & CFO

Marathon Oil

Cheryl R. Collarini
Energy Entrepreneur

Collarini Energy Staffing

Susan M. Cunningham
Senior VP Exploration
Noble Energy

M. Cathy Douglas
VP, Chief Accounting
Officer
Anadarko Petroleum Corp.

Kathleen Eisbrenner
Founder and CEO
Next Decade, LLC

Lynn Laverty
Elsenhans
CEO & President
Sunoco, Inc. and Sunoco
Logistics Partners LP

Samina Farid
Chairman
& Co-Founder
Merrick Systems

Meg Gentle
SVP and CFO
Cheniere Energy

Paula M. Harris
Director of
Community Affairs
Schlumberger

Barbara Heim
VP Human Resources
BG Group,
Americas & Global LNG

Kathleen A. Hogenson
President & CEO
Zone Energy

Barbara Lavery
Independent
Consultant/Executive
Coach

Karyl Lawson
Head of Energy
Practice
Phillips & Reiter, PLLC
and Founder of Women's
Energy Network

Gianna Manes
SVP and Chief
Customer Officer
Duke Energy Corporation

Laurie F. Markoe
President and CEO

Contract Land Staff, LLC

Rebecca McDonald
CEO

Laurus Energy, Inc.

Melody B. Meyer
President

Chevron Asia Pacific
Exploration and
Production Company

Peggy Montana
Executive VP,
Supply & Distribution

Shell Downstream Inc.

Sue Ortenstone
Executive VP & Chief
Administrative Officer

El Paso Corporation

Sharon M. Owens
VP of Corporate
Community

Centerpoint Energy

**Suzanne Paquin
Nimocks
Independent Director**
Encana

**Annise D. Parker
Mayor, City of Houston**

**Sue Payne
COO**
National Math &
Science Initiative
ExxonMobil

**Charlene A. Ripley
SVP, General Counsel
& Corporate Secretary**
LINN Energy

**Cecilia Rose
Executive Coach
Strategist**

**Maryann T. Seaman
VP, Treasurer &
Deputy CFO**
FMC Technologies

Cindy B. Taylor
President, CEO
& Director
Oil States International, Inc.

Jamie L. Vazquez
President
W&T Offshore

Martha B. Wyrsch
President
Vestas-American
Wind Technology, Inc.

Joan Eischen
Author
"Energy and the City"
Director, Advisory
KPMG LLP Houston

Chapter 3:
Build Your Personal Brand

There was a time when companies developed and directed careers for you. Today, few companies do this for you. They may move you around, but it won't be necessarily because they are investing in you. It is because they have a need and see you as the person to fill a role.

Cecilia Rose, a career coach strategist, says, "It is no longer sufficient just to be loyal to the company. You need to actively manage the development of your career, and create your own personal brand." Rose has over fifteen years of experience working as a trusted advisor and career and change management strategist with global Fortune 500 companies. She is a keynote speaker on topics such as "Who is managing your brand?" Rose explains that your personal brand is what differentiates you from the others on the team. Your brand will include your unique skills, successes and provide recognition as an expert. A brand should help develop credibility and a reputation within the company and industry. She suggests that you ask yourself what you are known for and what company can best help you build your brand.

Janet Clark, Executive Vice President and CFO of Marathon Oil, reminds us, 66 You do not have to accomplish everything in one day or one project; your professional reputation is something you build over time. 99

If you are at mid-career, you already have a brand, insists Rose. She asks: "Do you like it? Does it say what you want it to say? If not, change it, manage it, and create a different one." Protect your brand, because your reputation is at the heart of it.

Managing your brand and career are not singular events but a continuous process that must adapt to changing demands within the organization, the market, and you.

When protecting your brand and developing your career, sometimes you will have to follow your own strategy rather than doing what is convenient for others or for your company. One woman (who would prefer not to be noted on this story) was offered a lateral move into a business area of her company. Her boss tried to discourage her because she was an engineer and highly valued in her role; it was not a promotion she was considering but a lateral move. She wanted the role to try something new and was torn with the decision, because she did not want to disappoint a boss she liked.

In the end, she made the move and admits that it was the best thing for her career. She says that it was scary to move, especially because her boss did not help her with the process. The lateral move showed her another part of the business, and it allowed her to work on smaller projects that provided the freedom to do everything from the design to the delivery and getting the client to sign off on it. She interacted with business development and eventually landed a job in that department.

She is now in the C-suite of her company. She has a broad view on the business for her clients and a good understanding of what is required of her employees.

Develop an area of expertise

The future is bright, it's an exciting industry, and there are job opportunities in Houston, but there is still a ways to go. The latest statistics posted by the National Science Foundation noted that although the majority of university graduate students are women, the number of women enrolling in STEM (Science, Technology, Engineering and Math) graduate programs is still lower than the number of men enrolling in these programs.[2]

[2] http://www.nsf.gov/statistics/recentgrads, July 1, 2011.

People with technical degrees dominate the energy sector, and historically, women have been poorly represented in these technical degree programs. Advancement in the industry is more readily available to those who are educated in STEM disciplines; the women I interviewed say that when planning for college or graduate work, women should go with technical degrees. If you are not good in these areas focus on a specialization like accounting, economics or law. Avoid being a generalist studying just business. Having an area of expertise and a business degree will help you in the long run.

The industry is competing for new technical talent due to challenging and increasingly more complex resources. Technology for unlocking natural gas and oil from tight shale rock formation, drilling in deeper waters, and finding new alternative energy sources will require a technical workforce with deep expertise and knowledge. A significant part of the experienced workforce in the energy industry is aging and will soon retire, creating a mid-level gap. There are tremendous opportunities for women to take on leadership roles in technology and engineering. Graduating with good credentials and a technical degree will almost guarantee you a great opportunity in a major corporation.

Elsenhans, ranked number ten in Forbes list of powerful women in business, stresses the continuing need for scientists, engineers, chemists, and skilled workers that her company and others will need to replace the retiring workforce. As the first woman to head a major U.S. oil company, Elsenhans says, "Sunoco depends greatly on its scientists to optimize the use of oil, engineers to help make Sunoco's facilities safe and efficient, and process technologists to operate the company's equipment in an environmentally sound manner."[3] She initially dreamed of being an engineer or chemist but found that she did not have a strong talent for either field. She was good at math, so she decided to study applied mathematics.

In her role as CEO, she has the opportunity to mentor young, ambitious men and women who aspire to be part of the leadership team or lead a major part of the business. She says that success is something that everybody has to define for themselves. "If you want to run a business you need to have experience in the core areas of the business and understand how they make money," Elsenhans advises. She recommends that you learn how to create value, evaluate economics, and learn the financials. Learn to be a strong leader and supervisor, but be knowledgeable in your technical or operations area of expertise.

Within the STEM careers, there are many options to choose from. Susan Cunningham with Noble Energy was greatly influenced by a high school geography teacher. She originally started her studies in physical geography but then moved into mining geology. One of the first companies that Cunningham worked for gave her the opportunity to travel to North Africa as part of a project group. Being a woman in a male-dominated industry was not always easy, she admits. Cunningham says that in the energy industry, women are still not always taken seriously. She notes that in her travels to Africa, she quickly realized that the men in the government entity dismissed her. They thought she was the secretary, there to help the men.

Cunningham was determined to change their minds through her work. When they reviewed the data, she asked questions pertaining to the results, showing that she understood the business. In this manner, she exhibited her capabilities. Her hosts came to understand that she was indeed a geologist and a good one, equal or superior to the men in her company.

Like Cunningham, many of the women I interviewed tried to stay close to the operations of the company in line management during their entire career. Line managers are responsible for achieving the organization's main objectives by executing the key functions that generate revenue. In the energy industry this may include managing refineries or field offices, production sites and offshore rigs. Staff or administration managers support the operations side of the business in roles like accounting, legal, and personnel management.

[3] http://www.ccp.edu/site/news_room/press_releases/2009/093009pr.html, July 3, 2011.

I read that women today still make up the majority of staff and administrative positions. Some women are content and very successful in these jobs, but if you aspire to leadership in this industry, it is necessary to have 60 percent to 70 percent of your career in line management, working in the operations side of the business.

Many women take staff jobs because they like them. They are comfortable in and good at these jobs, but it is important to resist the pressure to stay in the roles if you want to lead a business unit. It is essential to be aware that staff jobs provide a different career path.

Melody Meyer with Chevron Asia-Pacific Exploration and Production Company is a mechanical engineer. She found her personal success and satisfaction in technical roles for her company. She says, "Always take on new opportunities and learn new things but stay true to your core roots and line management roles." Her advice is to not stray too far from your core function, especially in the early years.

Meyer held staff jobs from time to time and learned tremendously from them, but she resisted staying in them too long, because she enjoyed working in the field, close to the operations in a line management role more. "I like seeing a business perform and working directly with people to get that performance," Meyer says.

As a professional, being able to excel performing a staff function like marketing or commercial is valuable, but even the people who run functions have to have some experience in the field or line to ensure that they understand the business they support. You do not have to be an engineer to reach the pinnacle of success.

If you are not technical but interested to work in the energy industry, a host of other careers are available. This book is to encourage women to join us. In most companies there is a vice president for human resources, finance, commercial and accounting to name a few. First, define what success is for you. Young women are entering the energy industry with non-STEM degrees and learning necessary technical aspects on the job through commercial and management roles. This means you have to take some risks and take on projects where you are closer to the operations of the company.

Statistics are hard to find on the other areas of energy, but people are optimistic that women lead more and have a greater representation in alternative energy companies and power.

Sue Ortenstone with El Paso Corporation has a degree in civil and environmental engineering. She had a combination of line and staff roles during her career, but the majority of the roles she had early on were technical roles. She moved fluidly from leading engineering projects, business development, and corporate strategy to her current role with human resources and administration services. Ortenstone did say that in this industry, you need to have some technical affinity, or learn it on the job, to move up in an organization.

Remember soft skills

Most engineers or technicians do not study management and do not understand the importance of soft skills until it is too late (and detrimental to upward mobility). You will need to influence and motivate your team and bosses. Soft skills include good work ethics and attitude, listening, the ability to communicate across cultures and situations, critical thinking, personal drive, time management, and being able to work well with others on a team.

Without these skills, you may be stuck in a technical role that is fulfilling but may not get you where you want to be in your career. Without soft skills, it will be difficult to succeed in a management position.

It was mentioned several times that within the energy industry, it is essential to have deep technical or business knowledge and to be regarded as an expert in a specific area. In technical roles, soft skills can help you be successful working in teams and integrating ideas.

Many technicians do not understand that when you supervise others, it is no longer about personal performance or crunching numbers; it is about making others successful. Translate your success into their success. Acknowledge when they accomplish something and reach their goals. This is how you influence them and motivate them, not by the old methods of command and control. Help make everyone successful and heroes, and through them you will be successful. Listen more, ask questions, use humor, use visuals, keep some ideas open ended and seek closure on others, communicate, communicate, communicate—and laugh!

"Some lessons can be hard and are not always what you want to believe," says Halina Caravello, vice president for environment, health & safety. She told me that good relationships are much more important than technical knowledge. At first, that concept was difficult for her to accept, because she was a technical person by nature.

The engineers and people who tend to prefer science and technology are prone to value the technical aspects of an assignment more than they value the networking and communication skills necessary for team building. Relationship building is typically secondary for technical people. It can be hard for people who have spent so much of their lives acquiring that technical knowledge and level of expertise to learn something new.

Sometimes technicians feel shortchanged when they discover that to lead others, building relationships and communication skills are more important for management. Brilliant technical work can be reduced to nothing, because you did not communicate it well or you did not properly engage the stakeholders. Your work might be disregarded because of the way that you presented it. Everyone knows that technical knowledge is critical, especially early on. It is important to appreciate the different ways to communicate with others too.

It is a learning process for everyone including Susan Cunningham with Noble Energy. Throughout her career she focused on continuous improvement on the job and extended this mindset and process to her leadership style.

Early in her career, Cunningham was told by her peers and employees that she was often intimidating and assertive. That surprised her, because it was never her intent, but looking back, she confirmed that she was focused on getting the work done and trying to maintain reasonable hours. She recounted that having a child as part of a dual-career couple she felt there was no time for idle chit-chat. She thought that she couldn't spend time on "the personal side" if she wanted to get the job done. Her leadership style was focused on the task at hand, efficiency, and getting the work done so that everyone could go home at a decent hour.

Her family background set her up for this fact-based behavior. She grew up in a household of scientists and PhDs, where it was all about the scientific method. Her first leadership roles were all about presenting the facts; be objective and stay focused on the business. She says that when you progress into higher leadership positions, your focus should change to the people and building relationships with them.

I learned from many of the women I spoke with that it is important to connect with your employees so that you can learn what motivates them to get the job done. Examine all the possibilities for creating a high-performing team. People work for people, not companies, so it is beneficial when leaders understand what their team need to be efficient, productive, and committed to the company's success. Leading a team is more than a professional relationship. It helps to know more about your team members on a personal level and what their interests are outside the job. This information helps you motivate them and anticipate any shortcomings, and this requires strong soft skills.

Executive career strategist Cecilia Rose says, "One of biggest de-railers I have seen with my clients over the years is the blatant dismissal of soft skills that can also be referred to as interpersonal skills. I call soft-skills the 'invisible, critical skills.' The lack of these skills will detrimentally affect your career with regard to promotions, and leadership positions. The impact it has on the bottom line of the organization could stall a brilliant career or at least cause a setback. Technical skills may get you the job, but soft skills can make you or break you as a manager."

Whether you follow a technical trajectory or pursue human resources, marketing, IT, or law, without soft skills, your career may be stalled, derailed, or even ended.

Focus on job experience, not title

The best careers take advantage of opportunities, being in the right place at the right time, and being willing to take a chance. For young professionals in their first five years of a career, it is important to not fall into the trap of long-term goals.

Focusing on experiences rather than the job title will allow you to build your base of accomplishments to reach higher goals. Avoid the old-school thought of "where do you want to be in ten to twenty years." All the women I interviewed caution that such a mindset should be avoided. If asked this question, a good response is the following: "To continuously grow, to always be challenged, to look for opportunities, and to make the best of every situation." Have a long-term vision, but do your planning in smaller timeframes.

As you plan and build your career, think of it as a pyramid: the base of your work experiences needs to be bigger than the top or pinnacle, which is your area of expertise. Experts are made not born. Some individuals may be born with a certain talent, but that talent must be developed through practice. Your base is made up of all your roles performed and tasks completed at work that build your area of expertise that eventually defines your pinnacle of success. It is much more fun to practice the things that we like and do well, but real experts practice what they enjoy and add new skills and competencies to their base.

Kathleen Hogenson, president and CEO for Zone Energy notes that her first job after graduation was not the job she dreamed of when she was studying chemical engineering at Ohio State University. She graduated in the top of her class during tough economic times. What was important for her was to get a job in an energy company. She had the mindset that she would gain valuable experience in whatever role she received, learn from it, shine in it, and then earn the job she dreamed of.

In her job search, she started by determining what companies she wanted to work for that did not have a hiring freeze. She was advised to accept whatever role they had to offer, even if it was less than she had hoped for. It was great advice that worked for her, and she is certain that it is still sage words for any graduate looking for work in an economic crisis.

This advice landed her an entry-level job with great benefits in a publicly owned company that was part of a larger enterprise. The role allowed her to shine in front of all the right people. She worked in the corporate office, which allowed her to see how decisions were made and what was important in the projects they pursued. She was quickly identified as a high-potential talent and moved up fast. She started building a reputation (brand) of doing more than the job required.

Hogenson says that a "grooming role" allowed her to grow. She admits that she was a bit of a gopher but she did not care. She saw management going through the decision-making process, saw the technical teams present their projects, and heard what management cared about. She was building her base of experience and knowledge.

She stayed in this role for one year and then went into the field in an elevated role. Her new position brought her back to the corporate headquarters; presenting her findings to the same people she used to work for. She knew what to present and the information they needed to make a decision.

"Do not be afraid to start a bit lower than you dreamed. Sometimes a bit of luck and a lot of hard work is a great thing," Hogenson says.

Cathy Douglas, vice president, chief accounting officer with Anadarko Petroleum Corporation says, "If you get too set in your ways and have a predetermined path to follow, you may miss an opportunity along the way." Douglas started with Anadarko as a new hire because of the on-boarding program. At the time, she entered the rotational program, starting in the revenue accounting department. From there, she went to the general accounting department, tax accounting, property accounting, budgeting and planning, and financial reporting, and financial accounting. This path allowed her to see all areas of the business. Today, she has responsibility for all company functions including internal controls over financial reporting and risk accounting. She clarifies that she has not performed all these jobs, but due to the programs and career choices she made, she has had exposure to most of the areas within the accounting department of an energy company. These experiences built a foundation for her current role as the chief accounting officer, a C-Suite position.

Martha Carnes, partner, energy assurance with PricewaterhouseCoopers (PwC), is a CPA who took another route based on the experiences she wanted and the brand she wanted. She is a global subject matter expert in the natural gas industry. She works for one of the largest professional services firms in the world and has held many different leadership roles in her twenty-eight-year career.

At times throughout her career, Carnes contemplated moving into an energy company or manufacturer of goods and technical services for the energy industry, like two other women I interviewed. However, Carnes realized early on that she liked the dynamics of the service side because it has allowed her opportunities to meet many new clients in a variety of environments.

Carnes remembered that two years after graduation, she was given the opportunity to lead a team for a client project. The client asked how old she was, thinking she had to be in her early thirties, due to the amount of responsibility she had on the job. That made her realize that she was going to have more responsibility, earlier in her career that she wouldn't get working in an accounting department for a financial or energy company.

She enjoyed the many different opportunities her company had to offer her such as audit, tax, or financial advising within a particular industry. She chose to specialize in energy early on. Her company also allows for project work overseas and the opportunity to go on an expatriate tour and come back. They encourage their employees to take on those roles.

Carnes coaches young hires to have patience; it took her twelve years to become a partner, starting at the associate level. In the current environment, the normal route to becoming a partner is closer to fourteen years. She admits that it was a long time and took a lot of hard work along the way, but the exposure and learning was unique and worth the time involved.

A woman who took yet a different route is Cindy B. Taylor, president, chief executive officer and director with Oil States International, Inc. Early in her career, she worked for a public accounting firm, but after several years in public practice, she realized that she was missing the sense of ownership of a product or a company. She felt as though she was a consultant to many but owned nothing. Taylor saw the career path she was on and decided to change it.

The typical path for a multinational service organization is to be a partner in the firm, and Taylor recognized that it was not what she wanted. She liked the idea of leading her own company where she could feel as if she made a difference in the success and the development of a business, day after day.

Taylor made the career change when she had two young children. It was a time of reflection, and she asked herself questions such as "what do I want to do, what do I want my family life to be, and what do I want my career to be?" She says that sometimes you have to take a step back and ask these questions to find personal success and satisfaction.

Douglas, Carnes, and Taylor enjoy the people side of the business, but each took different routes. All three routes provided amazing careers for these women and an admirable image within the energy industry. They will tell you that your path depends on you, your career aspirations, and who you want to be. You may not get every step right at the beginning, but take a few moments to step back and analyze your experiences and direction. There is always time to adjust.

Douglas says that early on in your career, a lot depends on the size of the company and what the opportunities are for an accountant, or whatever discipline you have studied. Remember that titles vary from company to company. If you want self-esteem or self-identity from a title, working in a smaller company will be perfect for you, because it is easier to get senior leadership roles. In a Fortune 500 company, there are many levels to traverse before you hit the VP level or C-suite. Douglas advises researching what is available, checking out several companies, comparing, and then deciding.

How do you know who you want to be or what brand image you want to create when you are just starting your career or planning for college?

Consider the experiences you want to have in your life and career. The greatest experience the energy industry offers its employees is working and living internationally. The opportunity involves a level of risk and hard work for those who are willing and flexible to move. Sharing ideas with diverse cultures while working on projects or managing an international team will equip any new leader with skills for success.

Few people study engineering in order to manage people, but this is an option that will present itself in your career. It is wise to understand the direction these opportunities may take you. If you aim high in the organization, you will have to develop leadership skills. Is this something for you?

Some of the best technology and tools are developed in the energy industry. If you are interested in innovation and developing new ideas and methodologies, research and development might be the area for you. The energy industry is tasked with advancing technologies to resolve the environmental, supply, and reliability constraints of producing and using fossil resources. Resolving these constraints is critical to ensure reliable, secure, affordable, and environmentally responsible supplies. The industry needs fresh ideas that will lead in this direction. This may be a field of study for you.

Whatever path you decide to take, initially, you will have roles that are not highly visible or have relatively limited scope (for example, working in the lab or a smaller division within an organization). Volunteer for additional work on teams that are working in a critical area of the business like project management or try to get a role that is as broad as possible to give you more visibility in the organization. Get involved in high visibility projects so that others see what you are capable of.

"Do not be afraid to take a lateral move within your company; a move that is equal to or on the same level on an organizational chart as the former job," says Barbara Heim, vice president of human resources for Americas and Global LNG for BG Group. "Always consider lateral moves. Sometimes you have to actually take one step back to go two steps forward." Many of the women I interviewed took lateral moves and claim that this was part of their success. They built a broad base of knowledge of the company and operations that supported them in their leadership roles. Heim adds, "This does not mean jump at every opportunity. Remember, you have to define your goals and guiding principles."

Laura Buss Sayavedra, vice president and CFO for Spectra Energy Partners, LP encourages young people to make nonlinear, nontraditional career moves. She says that early on, it is okay to take risks and try new roles outside of your area of expertise. It broadens your thinking and teaches you what you like and do not like. Do not feel that you need to follow an engineering-only or finance-only career track. If you are an engineer, it's a good idea to learn more about the overall context of the business and seek out financial, operational, or commercial experiences. These skills will make you more valuable to your company, because you will be able to draw on diverse experiences as you move upward in the organization. Sayavedra says, "It is important early on in your career to take risks. Do something where you can leverage what you have done before but stretches you on new skill sets."

Take the path that provides a substantial level of responsibility, as what you do in a role is far more important early on. It builds the foundation for specialization. Cecilia Rose says, "It is like making a cake. Once you have the batter stirred up and the basics down, you can add different ingredients that will determine what kind of cake it becomes. Once a foundation is laid, it is easier for an expert to fold in other aspects to your expertise. This allows you to add value to what you have to offer."

Be your own advocate

Even with the success women have in the industry, some still struggle with expressing to company leaders what they need or what they want. The women that I interviewed agree that men do not have this problem. Some of the women suggested that young women worry too much about how they will be perceived in predominately male divisions (typically the technical areas in a company).

Linda Babcock and Sarah Laschever did a study at Carnegie Mellon. The study showed that even among men and women in their twenties and early thirties, men are much more likely to initiate negotiations than women.[4] They comment that whether they want higher salaries or more help at home, women often find it hard to ask.

Gianna Manes, senior vice president and chief customer officer for Duke Energy Corporation says, "No one else will take care of your career except you. Women need to learn to use their voices and make their requests known." She states that there are ways to ask that do not come across as pushy or demanding. Manes recommends that you let people around you know what kind of experiences you want in your career, and doors will open for you, but be realistic in your aspirations.

Laurie Markoe, CEO for Contract Land Staff LLC., says, "If you want that promotion, you have to ask for it. If you want to be the CEO, you need to let them know." She also says, "Be true to yourself, honor yourself, and be your own advocate." Markoe clarifies by saying that your requests must be in accordance with your experiences in the industry and time in the organization and that you must produce desirable results to be taken seriously.

Rebecca McDonald, CEO for Laurus Energy, Inc., shares a great example of how this approach worked for her. Early in her career, McDonald was working for an international engineering, procurement, construction and maintenance company. She discovered that the most interesting jobs in the procurement department were in the engineering construction division where the mechanical equipment was fabricated. At that time, the company did not have any female buyers and certainly none in the capital equipment or engineered product department.

McDonald went to the senior manager of procurement and asked to be a buyer trainee. He was an older gentleman and told her that he would have to get permission. He also told her that he did not mind because his experience showed that "women work twice as hard for half the credit." He said, "I would love to have someone who would work twice as hard."

[4] http://www.womendontask.com/authors.html, December 28, 2010.

Once you've done your homework, you need to ask for the job. McDonald did not initially plan to work in the energy industry, but she learned to look around her and discover the best place to be in the organization, according to her experience and skill sets. State clearly what you want, and tell as many key stakeholders within the company as possible. The women I interviewed used this principle in their conversations at work and with senior executives whenever the opportunity arose. Corporate decisions and succession planning do not always take place in the boardroom or in HR offices. They realized that opportunity presents itself in different ways. For example, two of five stakeholders may be traveling together when they begin discussing who should be the next VP of engineering or COO. It is critical that one or more of those stakeholders is aware of your areas of interest and is representing you. This is an example of sponsorship which will be addressed in the next chapter. It can have a profound impact on your career.

Know your audience when you make your requests known to your bosses and colleagues. There may be a fine line when voicing a request and that line is drawn in different places in different cultures in different companies. It is helpful to inject humor into a situation; it takes the edge off and makes the listener more comfortable. Have your antenna up as you are expressing your opinion or making requests. Be aware of how people are receiving your information and watch their body language. You need to test the waters, but do not get defensive or feel rejected or, worse, threaten to leave if they do not react immediately.

It is good to have ambition, but have it for the right reasons. That means having patience. The energy industry requires an understanding of the business, the clients, and the people you are working for, and this cannot be accomplished in a few years. Assess your readiness and the readiness of the company realistically. What is the typical timeframe for your company to promote individuals and offer them new experiences? For some companies, it is a set two-year rotation; for others, it is four years. Know your company's culture, and adjust your request accordingly. Building your credibility will get you far and open the doors to the conversations and the sponsorships you need to get ahead. Do not underestimate how much you need to know about this complex industry, and be prepared to answer questions.

Be aware that the situation may not be perfect. For example, there may be no promotions or roles when you are ready to move on or if you are not happy in a current job. Part of being your own advocate is taking charge of your career and managing your brand. It is up to you to make the best of a situation and figure out how to change it. Many of the energy companies I spoke with let employees know that they are in charge of their career and that help is available. Seek advice. People love to talk about what they do, and most of the time they are willing to help someone with career planning. Try to learn why you are not getting the roles and responsibilities you desire and then take action. Ultimately it is up to you to be proactive in your career planning. Seek out a mentor, and do not be shy.

> **A life spent making mistakes is not only more honorable, but more useful than a life spent doing nothing.** —Samina Farid, Chairman and Co-founder of Merrick Systems

Janet Clark of Marathon Oil says, "When you are ready to make the leap to the next level, do not just think about doing your job well enough to get the next promotion. Think about how you can go beyond what your job is or how your role is defined."

For example, if you are reporting to the CFO put yourself in the CFO's shoes and think about strategy. "You've got to be almost working at the level above you in order to get that position," Clark explains. This means that you gain perspective from your boss's view.

The women that I interviewed counsel young hires to learn how their job fits into the bigger piece of the business if they want to get to the next level. Apply an approach to a project based on the end result by asking questions earlier rather than later. Consider what is most critical—timing, quality or costs (for example). Do not get lost in the details and executing, because they will not highlight your leadership qualities. When you are lower in the hierarchy of the organization, you typically focus on details, so it is easy to forget the bigger picture. Ask for the context of the project and how it relates to what is required by you.

"Get outside of your box," Sue Ortenstone of El Paso Corporation recommends. Be confident, and raise the viewpoint rather than staying submerged in your task or function. Try to understand how your job or your group fits into the bigger picture. Is your group focused on growth because it is small? Is it a large division sometimes referred to as a cash cow? If you understand the big picture, such as how the company makes money, you'll learn how people make decisions and why the company drilled a well in Egypt rather than Kazakhstan. You will become a valuable player. Learn about the return on investment or ROI from well economics to the cost of capital. Emerge from the specific work you are doing, and add value to the overall project goal. Keep learning how to contribute more and be more effective. You may find a creative idea that moves the project in a better direction. Continuously learn and explore, and ask more questions.

Prioritize what you need to make the next step in your career. Take it on as an exercise with your manager. Assess your skill gap to understand where you lack knowledge and when you need support from those around you. Accept the fact that there are specialists who know more about their area than you will ever know. It may be your job to lead them and manage a project, because that is your strong set of skills. Establish trust and good relationships with your colleagues, and they will share with you their knowledge and experiences. The skills you need to hone will depend on the value your company places on each core competency. Find out what your skill set is and what you need to learn to advance, and develop an implementation plan.

Most companies work on a one year plan for their employees, setting your objectives in January. Around July or August, you have a review of where you are at with those objectives. This is a great opportunity for development; it is the time that you need to ask what your strengths are, where opportunities are, and what behaviors or skills you need to be promoted to the next job. At the end of the year, you should have an annual performance review that measures how you did against the objectives that you set.

The next step is a frank discussion over the findings of the gap assessment and what you need for the current job or potential next assignments. Make sure to get the feedback you need. Too often people assume that if they work hard and continue to get on projects, they must be doing well because no one has said anything negative. This is not necessarily the case; you are allowing the company to manage your career, and that should not be acceptable. Ask your boss what you can do better. Request a gap assessment at least once a year to keep your progress on track.

Cindy B. Taylor with Oil States International Inc. provides additional tips on how to develop a personal gap assessment. She says, "One of the best ways to gain personal insight is to put yourself in someone else's shoes and ask yourself how they would evaluate your skills. For example, mentally assume the role of a board member or CEO and list the skills that they would look for in a VP or president of a division. Once the list is complete, honestly evaluate your strengths. Where do you need to make improvements? Immediately, develop an action plan to fill in the gaps. "There is a whole host of things to do to actively manage your career. I think if you want to change how you do things, you have to make a conscious effort to reflect on what you are good at and where you could improve certain things or enhance your skills." Taylor suggests engaging a coach or mentor in the company who can help you in the process.

Meg Gentle of Cheniere Energy provides a good example of assessing career aspiration gaps and taking action to fill them. She was the manager of strategic planning for her company when she decided to attend Rice University to get her Executive MBA. She had no finance or accounting background and realized that she would have to study these areas. She says, "That is how I ended up in my current role. I assessed my knowledge gap and took advantage of an opportunity that ended up being so much more than I ever imagined."

Careers are built one step after another. Life changes, and sometimes, even the best laid plans can change. Take advantage of opportunities along the way, and rather than follow a path, create your own.

Consider company culture

If you are a recent graduate and new to the job market or you are thinking about changing companies, consider the company culture because it will be part of your personal brand. Employees need to fit with the style and personality of the company, as these aspects directly affect your career path. The energy industry is unique because it is male dominated, technical, highly visible, and political (it affects international relations).

Cathy Douglas is the vice president and chief accounting officer for her company. She says, "The culture of the company where you are contemplating to start your career, or moving to for a new role, should be considered. There are many different people in the world, and it is important that you realize you will be spending more than forty hours per week with them. Company culture affects how everyone interacts on a daily basis and is the foundation of how we educate and promote our people." What is meant by a "cultural fit"? During the hiring process, the company not only reviews your capabilities to do the job but also wants to make sure that your personality fits the organization. A mismatch could cause problems down the road, and an employee-employer match can mean the difference between job success and failure. If you cannot align yourself with a company, it is best to look elsewhere.

Douglas chose to work for a multinational oil and gas company, and she has been with the same company for her entire career. Working for an energy company was not what she planned when she was at college, but she chose that company over another multinational because she was able to participate in a rotational accounting program that was offered to new hires. She viewed this as an "investment in her." The on-boarding program fit her style of learning and the experiences she wanted to have as a new hire.

The best way to know the company culture is by working at a company. Speak with some of the new recruits at the company you are considering. Douglas suggests the following questions: What is the business model, and how does it generate profit? What are the values and missions? Ask yourself, "Do I really want to spend half of my day with this group of people, doing what they do?"

During the job interview, ask questions about the company's on-boarding program (do they have one?), how decisions are made, and what a typical career path is for the role you are interviewing for. If the interviewer cannot answer these questions, be wary. A company that has a defined on-boarding program is one that invests in your career.

As you are reviewing the company culture of a future employer, consider the dress code. Paying attention to dress code and making sure that it fits your style can make or break your career. How you dress speaks to what you want out of your career. All the women agree that men have a simple uniform, but women have a large range of options in attire, so they must be careful about what is or isn't acceptable.

Male-dominated industries present particular challenges for women's advancement because of stereotypes and gender bias. Attire can help you gain respect or lose it. Most people can find the correct outfit when a formal suit is required. The greater challenges are "Casual Friday "or a casual office environment. Avoid short skirts, low-cut necklines, too-high heels, too-tight clothes, and anything bordering on "too sexy." If you look like you are going on a date, to a nightclub, or the beach, don't show up at the office. You may be comfortable in your halter top or low-cut dress, but think of the people who want to work in a professional environment.

I asked the women I interviewed what they advised young women to wear. They all suggested an appropriate business wardrobe, meaning one that is adjusted to your particular workplace and office culture. If your office requires" business formal," a neat skirt or pantsuit, well-kept shoes, and minimal jewelry are appropriate. If you regularly work with clients or customers in person, be aware that you are a representative of your company, and choose clothes that are professional. Keep your hair and makeup simple.

If your office allows "smart business casual," then slacks and a blazer are a winning combination. This might be more formal than what your colleagues wear, but it is better for a woman to be overdressed than too casual. We never think poorly of a smart-dressed professional. Keep in mind that image is based on appearance, and women need to be taken seriously in the energy industry. Think about the image you have of the man who comes to work in a wrinkled t-shirt and flip-flops.

Laurie Markoe is CEO for her service company and recalls the first time she walked into a room full of high-level executives, all male. She was nervous, and she stuck out like a sore thumb as a woman in a sea of men in dark suits. The energy industry requires more somber, formal attire. Markoe notes, "As women, we each have to make decisions on our appearance and manners, depending upon how we want to be perceived, what helps us, what hurts us." She went through a phase of dressing like a man and wore a pantsuit every day. "That is not me," she says.

Markoe says that she has changed her attire to reflect her style and her feminine, personal brand. "When you walk into a room, and you are the only woman and you are dressed like a woman, it is an interesting place to be," she says with a smile. She does not shrink from the situation. Confidence is an important part of attire. If you don't feel confident wearing it, leave it in your closet.

Kathleen Hogenson, president and CEO of her own company, was twenty-two years old when she went offshore to work on a rig for the first time. Just out of college and with little money, she didn't have the right clothing for the job and no one informed her there was a particular uniform. She had the basics like steel tipped boots, overalls and a hard hat but hadn't planned for rain. Hogenson grabbed her Kelly green slicker and matching pink duffel bag, with Kelly green detailing, to use against the rain. She has long blond hair, and when she stepped out of the helicopter and onto the platform, one gentleman yelled, "Oh look, Barbie is here!" The crew teased her endlessly. All she could do at the time was laugh and respond with, "Yes, and I am looking for Ken."

She explains that typically men are respectful in this industry and usually do not say much, but that time, they couldn't contain themselves. She was young, and teasing her added some fun to the difficult and challenging work they were doing. Hogenson says that she bought a field raincoat for the next time she went offshore. Harmless mistakes will be made along the way in your career; if you add humor and correct them quickly, your professional image will not suffer.

Maryann T. Seaman, vice president, treasurer and deputy CFO for FMC Technologies says, "As the energy industry changes in terms of demographics, it will become easier to be a feminine woman, not just a woman. It is still a rough–and-tumble culture, so you need to have a tough outer shell and build a personal brand that is you but also takes the environment into consideration. A little bit of moxie will help along the way."

Chapter 4:
Sponsorship is Required for Advancement

In the interviews, we discussed the belief that women must have a mentor to get ahead in their careers. The results were split down the middle; many had mentors, most had sponsors, and a few participated in formal mentoring programs. All the women recommended mentoring when taking on a new initiative or new role at work, and they stressed that sponsorship is required to get ahead.

Lynn Laverty Elsenhans, of Sunoco Logistics Partners LP, tries to make herself available to both men and women for mentoring but feels it is a bit overrated. She says, "While mentoring is a great learning tool, sponsorship is the key to getting to the next level."

Elsenhans had several sponsors. She says, "The difference between a mentor and a sponsor is that a sponsor is willing to put their professional reputation on the line for you to give you a stretch assignment or recommend you for the job."

Break the Glass Ceiling with a Sponsor

High-performing women will not break the glass ceiling because they fail to acquire sponsorship they need to attain leadership positions, according to a Harvard Business Review research report.[5]

Despite gains in middle and senior management roles, women hold just 3 percent of the CEO positions in oil and gas companies. What's keeping women under the glass ceiling? High-performing women don't have the sponsorship they need to reach the top. Spearheaded by American Express,

[5] http://hbr.org/product/the-sponsor-effect-breaking-through-the-last-glass/an/10428-PDF-ENG, June 18, 2011.

Deloitte, Intel, and Morgan Stanley, the Hidden Brain Drain Task Force launched a study in 2009 to determine the impact of sponsorship and why women fail to make better use of it. The study found that women underestimate the role sponsorship plays in their advancement, and those who do grasp its importance fail to cultivate it.[6]

Elsenhans is visible in her role as CEO and has many people seeking her advice on how to get a sponsor. She explains that you do not get a sponsor; a sponsor chooses you based on your track record. She adds, "The biggest advice that I give women is to be willing to take stretch assignments; an assignment that you are not 100 percent sure you are qualified for. That will allow you to continually "stretch" yourself. The critical path is that you have to figure out how you are going to deliver the end results successfully and make sure you do. It is okay to make a mistake as long as you understand what you've done, you own up to it, you are accountable for it and explain what you've learned from it." Elsenhans found that having a mentor was extremely helpful during the stretch assignments in her career.

Annise Parker, Mayor of Houston, had a sponsor in her first job after college. Her boss had her learn about computers during the technology revolution. Her sponsor invested in the development of her technical skills, which eventually launched her career in the energy industry.

"I am forever grateful to her and try to give other young hires the same kind of break I was provided. It is important to recognize talent and reward it," Parker says.

Some say that women are not good sponsors for other women. There are several reasons why women don't sponsor other women, mainly because of time constraints from the work/life balance we will discuss in a later chapter. Also, some might say, that women are less likely to sponsor a woman who could surpass them and take the spotlight from them. Some limit themselves to sponsoring women with lesser ambitions, but when it

[6] http://hbr.org/product/the-sponsor-effect-breaking-through-the-last-glass/an/10428-PDF-ENG, June 18, 2011.

comes to someone with higher leadership potential that is valuable to the company, a senior female may shy away from sponsoring her.

Did you get a lucky break in your career? Luck, opportunity, and hard work all come together with a sponsor's help. If you had some great opportunities in your career, extend that lucky chance to other women and men in your organization and network.

Suzanne Nimocks, an independent board director, reaffirms that you need a sponsor to help you achieve your next promotion. "A sponsor and a mentor are two completely different worlds," she says. "A mentor is someone who can coach you, who can provide advice, who can be a supporter. A sponsor is someone who can create opportunities for you, someone who can be an advocate in the right environments with the right people."

Nimocks also recommends that you build credibility with several senior leaders because you never know when one may leave the organization. She says, "It is absolutely crucial, particularly in the early years when you have less visibility, to have sponsors. At that time in your career, you have less understanding of how your organization works, and you need someone who can help you navigate the network. A sponsor can create ideas for nontraditional leadership roles for you and help you create your career path."

When to use mentors

"Organizations must be cognizant and flexible to recognize the high potential [of women], especially if they want to capture their hearts and minds to grow them from junior positions into senior leadership roles," says Kathleen Eisbrenner of Next Decade, LLC.

When Eisbrenner went to work for a large multinational, she had for the first time an opportunity to mentor a group of women. She had always wanted to share her experiences and lessons learned with younger women. She recognized that the young women in the company were going through some of the same challenges she did early on in her career, and she met with them monthly over a two-year period. They talked about issues, business, and what excited them about the industry and their company.

"Don't underestimate how willing executives are to share," Eisbrenner says. "The natural development of a person is for giving and taking. You may be pleasantly surprised how willing senior people are to help others." What Eisbrenner didn't expect was the reaction she received from the men. She advises anyone leading an internal mentoring group to be aware of the perceptions of others and make sure to communicate clearly your objectives and motives.

> **"We are blessed to be a blessing to others and to share our gifts."** —Karyl McCurdy Lawson heads the energy practice at Phillips and Reiter, PLLC and is the founder of Women's Energy Network

When Samina Farid of Merrick Systems was promoted into a senior leadership role (replacing her boss who was a dynamic and successful man), she was concerned that she would not get the level of respect and support from the team she was hired to lead. Farid discussed her concerns with her mentors, and they reminded her that she was put in the role because she was capable and had the experience and qualifications it required.

Through this mentoring experience, Farid learned to lead. She struggled in the beginning, but after she got past worrying about being compared to her ex-boss and started focusing on the business issues and how to resolve them, her decision making and relationships with the team members started improving. She used her mentors to build her confidence along the way.

Halina Caravello is a vice president for her company and says that women need to ask for a mentor and not wait for one to be assigned officially through the company. She informally mentored women at her global company via email, phone, and face-to-face meetings. She recommends,

"Mentees have to be the ones who go and initiate the contact and keep it going. They shouldn't expect their senior executive mentor to always have the time to keep in touch."

Caravello was aware that many companies have formal mentoring programs, but typically they do not include everyone. It may not be possible to have mentors for every young hire who wants one, but she says, "If you are not selected for the formal mentoring program, that should not stop you from seeking one out."

Be a good protegée

Barbara Lavery, an independent consultant and executive coach, specializes in developing individuals who are in emerging leadership positions or are in major change agent roles. She has worked for numerous Fortune 500 companies. Lavery says, "Women without mentoring and sponsorship are at a disadvantage. Our male counterparts have a large pool of successful males with whom they can bond and learn. People who do not have these connections and networks sometimes seem to be lacking in organizational savvy. Without assistance, it's easy to retreat into a belief that hard, persistent individual contribution will be all that's needed for recognition and advancement. Mentors help us accelerate learning through the sharing of their experiences and providing access to people in their professional networks. Sponsorship gets us the stretch assignments that will establish our potential."

Sponsorship is more strategic and less developmental than mentoring. Sponsorship looks at what can you do for the company, whereas mentoring is about developing you as a person. In the early years of your career, it is important to attract a helpful mentor who could potentially sponsor you. A mentor is not always a sponsor but can help you in the first promotion and stretch assignment. Lavery offers these tips:

- Actively seek the mentors you want. Think about some specific goals you have and/or skills you want to master. Who could be most helpful?

- Stay true to the commitments you make to your mentor. Keep to the time and topic.
- Seek mentors who are good coaches. Just because someone is good at her job doesn't mean she is good at teaching. Sometimes the people who are most different from you can push you in new directions.
- Look at mentors as potential sponsors. They need to be well connected and respected within the organization.

It is also important to learn to be a great protégée.
- Ask for specific actions you can take. Who else might you talk with? What reading might be helpful?
- Be an active listener. Ask good questions and listen for deep understanding and the emotions beneath the words.
- Stay action oriented. When a valued mentor makes a suggestion, act on it and reflect on the impact.
- Ask for help before a stretch assignment; one that requires a leap beyond your comfort zone.
- Give the mentor feedback. Let her see the value she is providing.
- Be appreciative. A great mentor is a gift that should never be taken for granted. Let her share and celebrate your successes.
- Reach out to more than one mentor. Many successful leaders form a personal board of directors. Some members may invest in an active relationship, and some members may contribute upon specific and limited requests.

Observe good leadership

The women I interviewed didn't have mentors early on in their careers. They looked to people whose judgment they trusted and tried to spend as much time with them as they could, because they knew they could learn from them. They were the role models who they observed at crucial times in their careers. Martha Wyrsch saw one of her mentors switch from the legal profession to running a business. Wyrsch saw the possibilities and now is a president for a global corporation.

Observing successful senior leaders can be the best way to learn how to act and behave, especially if you don't have a mentor or sponsor. The women remind us there was little focus on developing talent or leadership when they started their careers, so they learned on the job from their bosses and colleagues.

Sue Ortenstone, with El Paso Corporation, had a boss who was a fabulous leader on the business side. He taught her to reason using data and to leave emotions out of the discussion. Ortenstone is a high-energy person, so she could come across as passionate for a project, which others may have defined as being emotional. She advises young women that by using data in a presentation, the conversation becomes logical. "If you get pulled into an emotional discussion, you aren't going to get anything accomplished."

Ortenstone learned good leadership skills by watching how her boss treated others. She noted that he was collaborative, listened well, wanted feedback from others, always got opinions, never raised his voice, and had a lot of energy. He sought input especially in contentious issues but remained level headed.

In her previous role as a geoscience resource manager for ExxonMobil Exploration Company, Sue Payne led over fifteen hundred technical resources. She described her leadership style as "trying to be a good example for others to follow." Think about how her style could be adjusted or adapted for your learning experiences.

Payne tries to set expectations that raise everybody's game and the quality of work that is the end result. She tries to help her team find their own style within their roles and projects. She steps back from the day-to-day tasks to allow her team the freedom and latitude to explore their creativity and complete a job in their unique way.

She has a weekly team call with her group, and sometimes there are individual calls with key players for a project. They discuss the project and talk through any challenges, and she encourages them to think through the process by asking questions. Payne prefers the weekly calls to email because it gives a personal touch, it's easier for her to discern if there are problems, and it allows other members working on similar (or different) projects to learn from each other. She uses these opportunities to mentor her team.

Her direct team consisted of 8-10 direct reports and there were younger women, older men, and anyone in between, including people of different races and cultures. "Allowing them to explore their own style and share information promotes cross-pollination, and they often learn from each other, which is when the job gets fun," says Payne.

Build your network

Everyone tells you that you need a network, but few tell you how to do it and, worse, no one tells you why. Anyone you meet can be in your network, but keeping your network alive is the key. An active network can be used to get a mentor or sponsor, look for a job, seek advice, and offer help to others.

There was a time in Houston when few woman executives worked in the energy industry. Trying to find a mentor, a sponsor, or even a female friend was not easy. Karyl McCurdy Lawson heads the energy practice at Phillips and Reiter, PLLC, and she is the founder of Women's Energy Network (WEN). She moved to Houston in 1988 and, not knowing where to meet other professional women, immediately felt the isolation. A friend recommended that she participate in Leadership Texas, a program offered by the Foundation for Women's Resources and the longest-running women's leadership program in the United States.[7]

Lawson found it to be a powerful program, because it focused on having successful women as speakers in substantive areas as well as leadership development. She says, "When you see someone who looks like you and shares your issues and has success, you think I can do that too." Lawson remains in contact with many of the women who are part of her network.

She used the successful example of Leadership Texas to solve her female networking issues in Houston by starting WEN, an international association for women professionals that provides networking opportunities for women in the energy industry and fosters career and leadership development.[8] WEN is over nine hundred women strong and is a great resource for learning how to network and get a mentor. WEN offers an annual mentoring program that focuses on the issues of leadership and advancement for young women. Many of the young women are building a personal board of directors from the contacts they make at WEN. A personal board is a collection of people who know you well professionally, are interested in your well-being, and have useful points of view.

When I arrived in Houston in early 2007, I volunteered and served on the WEN board of directors for three years; it was the best way to get exposure to energy companies and industry leaders. It introduced me to an amazing network of women that still flourishes today. I recently changed companies, and it was due to the contacts I made at WEN.

Job search networking is still the best way to find a new job. Like I did and many of the women I spoke with, Laurie Markoe, with Contract Land Staff, obtained many of her jobs through her personal network. Markoe comments that most of her sponsors were found through her network and some eventually became her boss or colleague.

Networking can also mean within your company. Get to know other groups outside of your division. Move from one group to another through lateral moves. Take time to go to lunch with your contractors, the people in the office, and colleagues working in the field. These people may have an impact on what you do or an area of the business that you may affect. See these as potential positions; the information will provide you with a broader knowledge base, allowing you to reach out to your colleagues and peers for new perspectives. This is a form of mentoring that may result in a sponsorship in a new role or division.

[7] http://www.womensresources.org/LT.asp, November 17, 2010.
[8] http://www.wenhouston.org, November 17, 2010.

Sharon Michael Owens, vice president corporate community relations with Centerpoint Energy had a mentor early on who advised her to "mix it up a bit" and encouraged her to get to know a broad variety of people. Her mentor advised her to be careful who she associated with: "As women, we tend to spend too much of our time with other women." It is a natural instinct to want to mix with others who look like you or share your cultural experience. An association like WEN is a great place for women to build one of many networks. Diversity in your network is important. Owens recommends that you look at networking based on interest, areas of expertise, and cultures. Diversity is not just based on race, ethnicity, or gender. Get to know a variety of people within your work setting and industry.

66 We will know we are successful when every employee starts their day with a sense of purpose and ends their day safely with a sense of accomplishment. 99
—Martha Wyrsch, President of Vestas-American Wind Technology, Inc., North America

Chapter 5:
Make the Shift from Team Player to Leader

Knowing your value comes with having a crystal-clear understanding of what you do uniquely and well in your organization. Women need to maintain their confidence levels when they are in leadership positions. Unfortunately, from time to time, especially in a male-dominated industry, women question whether they got the job because of gender. This undermines confidence right away, even before they get to start in the role.

Women (and men) torture themselves with thoughts of failure that play over and over in their heads. Women can struggle more when they are the "only girl" in the room, when they work in a male-dominated industry, and when they are the only engineer in a group of guys. Barbara Lavery states that "mental tapes" are the messages we hear and internalize, sometimes without much critical thought. Typical messages that affect how we feel about ourselves as leaders include the following:

- Over-reaching ("Just who do you think you are, little missy, thinking you deserve this or belong here").
- Exclusion ("Engineering is for men. We do not expect women to be successful in technical roles").
- Organizational doubt based on previous experiences ("We invest in women, but they leave to have babies")
- Inconvenience ("We have to make special accommodation for you").
- Novelty ("You know this team has never had a women leader before, we aren't sure how they will react").

When you hear these messages, you can use them as teachable moments. Do not be discouraged. Decide if the message is coming from others or if it is a "fear tape" being played in your own head. Successful mentors should be able to help you see yourself as others see you. At some point, successful women find a way to retire the tapes, and this opens a door to courage. That suggests that while self-doubt holds you back, it also keeps you safe. What would you be doing now if you gave yourself permission to reach for it?

The advice I heard in the interviews was to "not worry about rumors, because the hallway talk doesn't matter." The company is not giving you a job because you are a female but because you earned it.

Leadership can often happen quickly through a rapid ascension — suddenly you are leading colleagues. Several of the women I spoke to were promoted one or two levels above their peers. They were promoted because of their technical skills and often found they were the only woman in a management role leading teams of men. Without a female role model, they had to develop their management style based on their surroundings, which sometimes created insecurity and a lack of self-confidence and leadership.

One woman recalls a particularly difficult time in her career. She had been promoted quickly, up two levels, surpassing her friends at work. She remembered this clearly because people were suddenly uncomfortable with her as their boss and maybe uncomfortable with her success. Her leadership style tended to be more "feminine," and she had difficulty with the other women on the team who treated her with some unexpected behavior. Rumors started quickly about why she was promoted, and she was left out of the weekly lunches and internal network.

If you find yourself in this situation, it is crucial not to be intimidated. Changes did not happen overnight, but she stuck to it and started behaving like a boss. She decided to be fair and reasonable with the people who were challenging her and not take any nonsense. She kept her manner very businesslike and professional, and eventually people realized that she got the job because of her superior technical skills. The rumors stopped. She started to build a network at her new level and interacted with her employees as a boss. She earned their respect and, in the end, their friendship.

> **❝Acknowledge and move on. ❞**
> —Laura Buss Sayavedra
> Vice President & CFO
> Spectra Energy Partners, LP

Peggy Montana of Shell Downstream, Inc. wants women to know that she has been in many human resource conversations over her twenty years and has never once heard anyone say that they were going to give a job to an unqualified person or an unqualified woman.

Step into the leadership role

Women think that they need to understand everything as soon as they walk into a job rather than learn and the various aspects on the job. Do not shy away from your first leadership role. Montana says, "Act your way into it. Create a mental model of being the boss and being comfortable as the leader."

She will never forget her first meeting as the leader of a new team. Her boss stepped into the discussion to set the direction and give orders. Afterward, she discussed this with him, and he told her that she needed to step into the leadership role or he would do it for her. Montana did step forward and is now an executive vice president.

Women continue to ascend to positions that were previously designated as "male" roles. They are leading within their companies and leading men. Montana replaced a man in the job when she took her first management role in production. The man she was replacing was concerned that she would not be accepted; he thought he was doing her a favor by walking the production area and talking to all her new direct reports. His conclusion was that she would be accepted as the boss in this traditional role with all male employees. He informed her that "the guys were okay with working for a woman."

> **"** Challenge yourself. Taking on the more difficult tasks and being successful builds your ability and confidence to take on even bigger assignments. **"**
> —Peggy Montana, Executive Vice President for Supply and Distribution, Shell Downstream, Inc.

She did not take offense. She realized that having the buy-in from her staff was critical for her success. Although the employees didn't have a choice about whether the boss was a man or woman, she was glad to know that everyone accepted her as the boss.

A great way to gain confidence in a new role is to listen. Your manager won't expect you to know everything at the start of your career or the start of a new role. Take the time to absorb information and learn. Many of the women I interviewed came into the workforce at a young age and managed people who were older. The worst thing a new hire can do is to tell everyone that "you can do it better." That may be true, but deliver that message carefully. Listening to other generations and their ideas is important. Do not make generational assumptions such as "they are too old to understand new technology." As many of the women interviewed mentioned, listening is the key to being accepted as a leader.

Melody Meyer with Chevron focuses on the value that comes from change in order to present new ideas that may not be popular at first. Meyer grew up in the oil patch with a father who was a senior petroleum engineer. She never hesitated to roll up her sleeves and do what was needed to be done, and she did not let roadblocks or old attitudes get in the way. She listened to the people with experience in the job and valued their input.

Meyer remembers that her first supervisory job was when she was twenty-four years old. At that time, drafting was done by hand. Her boss asked her to supervise the drafting department and convert it to computer-aided design and drafting (CADD). She had eight direct reports, all who had about twenty-five years of experience.

To make the transition to CADD, the group members had to take typing lessons, which were considered "secretarial skills" at the time. Meyer admits that they eventually accepted the task, because they all saw that it was necessary to be productive. They made the conversion quickly and raised the performance level, so it was easy to get everybody on board.

The other lesson she learned about change was: "Make a goal everyone's, not just your own. Inspire and lead your group through actions."

Less-experienced employees are anxious about meeting expectations with the additional responsibilities they assume as they move up the organization. There is no shame in asking for assistance. Do away with pride, and show respect for the talent that others bring to the table. There is no such thing as a single-handed success. When you are leading and working toward common goals, it is important to include and acknowledge the talent on your team.

Delegating can be difficult for any new leader. It requires a change in perspective, and it is important to let go of the idea that you can do it better. Delegating does not mean abdication. Most people struggle with delegating because it "costs time to teach others when you know you can do the job." If you are going to grow, to let go of doing everything yourself, you must leverage the talents of others. This is where many new leaders fail. When leaders spend too much time on the details they lose the ability to lead, which causes their followers to lose confidence and trust.

> 66 Leadership starts with three passions: honesty with yourself, wanting to get projects done, and ensuring the success of others. 99
> —Jamie Vazquez, President, W&T Offshore

Many young people worry how delegating will reflect on them. A well-thought-out system for delegating and following up with your people will take the uncertainty out of delegating. Here is an example of a plan that may help you overcome micromanaging.

Suzanne Nimocks, is a recently retired Director (senior partner) in McKinsey & Company's Houston Office. She acknowledges that in the beginning of her career, she made a lot of mistakes in terms of delegating. She wanted to control all the details. Her team gave her

feedback and requested that she allow them to come up with some
of their own conclusions.

As a senior manager and partner for the firm, Nimocks was leading
complex consulting projects. She started learning how to test people early
on and created an environment where she could encourage them to ask
questions. She wanted to accomplish tasks without eleventh hour surprises.
She was not someone who believed in working in crisis mode all the time.
Nimocks implemented the following steps in varying degrees, depending
on the size and complexity of the project. She balanced two conflicting
needs: space for the team to perform and assurance that high-quality
projects were being delivered on time.

She developed a work plan with her team, often over lunch in a
nonthreatening environment. She asked how they felt the project was
progressing, if there were any surprises, and what adjustments they
needed to make. She had the younger hires walk through their work plan
out loud. She confirmed that in an oral discussion, people develop the
ability to test their own knowledge and judgment and build confidence
about the approach they were taking, as if they were convincing themselves
or confirming their thesis.

Nimocks defined an exhaustive list of intermediate milestones so that she
could regularly keep track of the progress without interfering with the team
or seeing surprises at the end of the project. She focused on the key issues
and led her associates toward a synthesis at various points of the project.
This avoided overdevelopment of research and kept the team from moving
in the wrong direction. She asked the team to develop five "sound bites"
to deliver to the client—this is often referred to as an "elevator speech"
(succinctly deliver the status of the project as if you were to step into
the elevator and find yourself riding up several floors with the client).
Her team developed a chart each night, prior to leaving the office that
synthesized what they knew, as though they had to finish the engagement
that day. Nimocks wanted them to realize that the issues were in constant

development, renewing and changing, but that it was important to put the pencil down and synthesize regularly. Without this step, they could analyze forever without achieving closure.

Finally, Nimocks asked the team to write an outline of the final presentation early on to ensure that the logic was tight and to avoid unnecessary churning. This outline was regularly reviewed and updated, and it formed the foundation for the final work product.

These are the steps that Nimocks implements in her leadership that prevent her from having last-minute surprises while still giving the team space to work. "I integrate lots of different moments for analyses with the team and the communication between us," she says.

The key to delegating, or controlling your desire to micromanage, is to keep your hands on the controls of the steps that will hurt someone or stop business, but for everything else, lighten up. People learn through mistakes and the consequences of their actions. Mistakes are opportunities for positive feedback on how they could do the job the next time or to advise the person behind them. Use them as opportunities to refine your coaching and leadership skills.

Sue Payne, COO for the National Science and Math Initiative representing ExxonMobil, says that she never wants to hear herself say, "This is how I do it, and you have to do it this way, too." Payne believes that the way to ensure a team's success is to let the team play. Set broad enough parameters to allow people to enjoy the job, support them with time and attention, and make sure that they understand how their work is important to the overall success of the company.

Jamie Vazquez of W&T Offshore advises women to seek management training when taking a leadership role or have a formal plan prior to leading a team. She was twenty-seven when she led her first team and admits that the experience did not meet her expectations. She associates this with a lack of available management training at the time. Vazquez says that no matter what role you are in, whether you are moving to CEO or leading a new team, every change requires a transition period.

Toot your own horn

Attitude and presentation become important when you are ascending the career ladder. Learn to have "presence" as a leader and not be stereotyped as a woman but as a leader.

Janet Clark, executive vice president and CFO for her company admits that many women, including her, often do not take credit for their success. Like many other women, Clark recognizes that "some tend to acknowledge the team rather than individual accomplishments."

Clark suggests that when you complete a big project, giving the team credit is critical, because you would not have accomplished it without the team She advises, however, that when you talk about the project, make the role that you played as a leader clear. Articulating this in a thoughtful way allows people to realize that you were the architect for the project. There is no need to use the word "I" or draw too much attention to your own work. It is a fine line to walk, because no one likes to hear people who talk only of their own success. It is particularly difficult for women to find the right level of assertiveness. When women are passive about their success, they are considered "soft," yet if they are straightforward or assertive, they are often labeled "brash" (or worse).

If you are interested in moving up in an organization, learn your value and the strengths that you bring to the table. Samina Farid of Merrick Systems spoke of the young women who had worked for her in previous companies (or now in her own company) who failed to promote their accomplishments and skills. She reminds us that no matter how qualified or competent you are, you will not get promoted through hard work and effort alone. Find your style, and toot your own horn.

Farid told the story of a soft-spoken, smart young woman with a master's degree who worked on a team made up of mostly men. She was so soft-spoken that when she said something, the men talked over her or ignored her comments. Farid noticed that this young woman often had astute comments, but she wasn't able to express her thoughts around her much louder, assertive male colleagues.

This bothered Farid, but she let it go for a few days to see how the situation developed. When things didn't change, she explained to the young woman that when she allowed the men to talk over her, they were missing out on the opportunity to hear her observations. It was important for the young woman to understand that to be part of the team she would have to figure out a way to participate as an equal.

The next day, when she started to present her idea and someone interrupted her, the young woman firmly looked at him, said, "Excuse me, I am not finished," and went on to complete her comments. Another time, she laid her hand on her male colleague's arm and asked him to be quiet until she finished. He listened to her, and so did the rest of the group. It didn't take long until the team respectfully listened when she talked. She took control of her manner and did this in such a way that she felt good about herself. The men on her team treated her as an equal, and she flourished as a professional.

Farid says, "It is not about changing who you are but working with what you have and having fun while you are doing it. You have to establish equality and understand the importance of each situation and consider the culture."

Say it with conviction

In addition to "finding your voice," you need to be heard, and many women consider this to be a challenge. It is not that they do not have opinions or something to say—they are afraid of rejection or intimidation. Part of being a valuable employee is sharing your ideas, objections, and opinions. You deserve the opportunity to express yourself, and once you find your voice, you need to speak up and give your message.

Melody Meyer is president for Asia-Pacific for her company. She advises all new hires that being an effective communicator is important in leadership. Early in her career, she joined Toastmasters to learn to be a stronger communicator. She has started a Toastmasters organization in every country she ever worked. "It's essential to push yourself to continually learn and improve your personal skills throughout a career," she says.

Several of the women I interviewed told stories of being "the only woman in the room" early on in their careers and how difficult it was sometimes to present their ideas and be recognized for their contributions. When you are the only woman and you present an idea, men may talk over you like we heard before from Samina Farid. When you make a comment, they may ignore it. When someone else mentioned the idea later, he may claim it. When that happens, you have to take ownership. You can say, "John that is interesting. I heard that before because I mentioned it." Reclaim the idea and own it. Take the idea you presented to the next step or provide the solution that you had in mind. Once you claim it, continue to develop it. Humor is a great way to get your point across. Practice your delivery so that it sounds natural and not defensive.

Charlene Ripley, senior vice president, general counsel and corporate secretary for LINN Energy needed to find her voice, literally. After an important promotion, she realized that her communication style had served her well in the past, but her new direct reports claimed that they often did not understand what she wanted or expected. Ripley is Canadian, and Canadians are generally less direct than Americans, but she also wondered at the time whether the problem could be "a female thing."

She started to read about the different styles women and men use to communicate in business. She considered how she conveyed written and verbal information. Ripley says, "When you are the only female in a meeting with men, you need to be heard and get their attention so they do not wonder why you were invited to the table."

She realized that her communication style needed to change. She hired a coach and paid for coaching services. She knew that it was a good investment in her career and recommends that others to do the same.

Ripley focuses on providing good legal support in her role as senior counsel. As part of the management team she believes it is important that she demonstrates an understanding of the business and provide general leadership. She emphasizes the importance that you speak at a meeting, even when the topic is not a core area of what you do at the company. Do not be afraid to ask questions. It shows that you are engaged and you want to use this information in your job.

She remembered when it wasn't always easy to ask questions or speak up in a meeting. When she was young, she was part of a leadership team in a company that consisted primarily of older men. She met with them every Monday morning in the CEO's dark, wood-paneled office. The first twenty minutes of the meetings were spent talking about football games and hunting trips, topics about which she had little to contribute. After that, they went to the weekly report.

Those meetings were intimidating for her, but she was determined to get through them in an effective and professional manner. She practiced the delivery of her report over the weekend, like a CNN reporter delivering crisp news reports. The next Monday, she emulated the reporter while delivering her weekly report. She received two emails from men on the board congratulating her on her message and professionalism she exhibited.

However, she still felt like an outsider. Her next step was researching the important interest of her management team, and that was college football. On Sunday nights, sitting with her husband, she studied the outcomes of all of the college football games. She was soon able to comment on who won or lost and learned enough to discuss particular plays and player performance. Ripley showed interest in what the group enjoyed, and eventually she had fun attending the Monday morning meetings. She learned a valuable lesson about gaining trust and winning people over.

A company culture that encourages the participation and involvement of its members is one of the most important assets of an organization. In a survey of America's top thirty-four firms, it was found that most financial indicators like sales growth, return on investment, and customer satisfaction are better in companies that have a participative culture.[9] Executive teams that lead these organizations bring their past experiences, energies, and personalities to the table.

These conversations and interactions are changing as more companies add women to the board and leadership teams. During my interviews, I heard that sports, hunting, and fishing are still the pastime and entertainment for many of the leading boards in Houston. As women, we need to change the conversations. When female board members and managers build relationships and can speak with confidence, trust develops. Being able to find your voice and speak out is a critical part of being a leader in your company.

Make a decision

Finding your voice and speaking out requires making decisions. Have no doubt. Some women struggle with this. When you are in a leadership role, it is important to be decisive and express your ideas. This doesn't mean having a closed mind or not seeking advice from others. Develop a sense of timing for the decision, and know when to stop gathering information and building consensus.

[9] http://www.slideshare.net/denisonconsulting/denison-organizational-culture-model-overview,The Denison Model, Vol. 1, Issue 1, 2006.

Sue Ortenstone of El Paso Corporation talks about her experience of moving from being part of the team to leading it. "When you become a manager, people think you get smart overnight. Well, you do not." Ortenstone says that you are the same person but with a new title. However, your team will look at you for answers and for decisions.

Martha Wyrsch of Vestas-American Wind Technology, Inc. notes that in decision making, too many people want to ensure that they have dotted all the i's, crossed all the t's, and done all the research, when 80 percent of the information is usually good enough to make a decision. "You have to be very confident in yourself and in your intuition," She says. "One thing that I have learned is that you can study too long. You have to make a decision to move, and do it. Business becomes stagnant if you do not."

Paula Harris, director of community affairs with Schlumberger, remembered the first time she was someone's boss. "It is kind of overwhelming as a new field engineer and it is very overwhelming for a young female field engineer," she says. Harris acknowledged that at first she was insecure; she was fresh out of college and had older men reporting to her, asking her for direction and guidance on a project.

Harris is a consensus builder. She uses leadership skills in her role at work and as an elected official for the Houston Independent School District. In the past, she explained everything; she wanted everyone's input and most important, she wanted everyone to be happy. It took some time to realize that she was "on the line" as the manager and that she needed to make final decisions based on the input she received. "If you do not make the final decision, you will diminish your leadership role," she says. "Whether something goes right or something goes wrong, you are responsible." She shared a first-time leadership story. Harris started as a field engineer, gathering data and providing technology for oil companies, so she wore a hard hat, the steel toes, and the coveralls. When she arrived on the offshore rig, 99.9 percent of the time she was the only female and the only African-American on the rig. The rigs were not designed for women, so she either slept in a hospital room or her peers would have to move and sleep together to allow her a private room.

When she arrived on the rig, she heard an announcement, "Woman on board, woman on board," and everyone ran around to prepare the facilities for her. She didn't like all this attention.

At that time, she heard, "Women don't belong out here" or "No one told me a woman was coming." Harris says she wanted to hide from that at first. After a few operations, she started to gain her self-confidence and learned to manage situations on the rig. She started to assert herself as a leader. She started to take charge and make decisions, telling her direct reports and colleagues where she wanted to stay and who to move to accommodate her. She came to understand that she was there to do a good job and that she needed special facilities.

When she heard the men's comments, she replied, "You do have a woman on board and you have a good one, so let's do the job we are all here to do."

Harris grew in her leadership role and learned to make decisions and not question them. However, she still liked to have the people around her happy. She reflected on her experiences and remembered that some people were never happy. It took some time for her to realize this and not let them sabotage the good work she was doing. She asserted herself as the leader and took on decision making, realizing that some would never agree, and moved on to the next issue.

Annise Parker, Mayor of Houston, learned over her twenty-year career in energy how to instill a sense of urgency. She worked for a family-run business, and when the executive team wanted information, they wanted it then and now. Data was gathered and presented, a decision was made, and then action was taken.

She found that the pace of government was tremendously different than her previous company in its decision making. There is a long vetting process. Parker does her best to instill a sense of urgency. She says, "The world is changing around us, and we need to keep up with it. We gather information; make informed decisions, act, and move on to the next issue. We try not to spend a lot of time agonizing over something."

Kathleen Eisbrenner in Dubai with Qatargas.
Photo courtesy of Royal Dutch Shell plc, 20 April 2008.

Cindy B. Taylor reviewing a Noble blow out preventer transporter system.

Samina Farid
with State Senator
Rodney Ellis as part
of a delegation
organized by
the Bilateral US-
Arab Chamber of
Commerce in the
Middle East
(May 2010).

Peggy Montana at the Chuquicamata copper mine in Calama, Chile.
Shell Global Supply & Distribution provides all the fuel to the mine
operator from a nearby terminal.

Martha Wyrsch getting a bird's eye view on top of a Vestas wind turbine with her VP for health & safety and field technician.

Karyl McCurdy Lawson receiving an award from former WEN President Rachel Giesber Clingman commemorating the 10 year anniversary.

Sue Ortenstone and her team: Cindy Sebald- VP, HR, Joan Gallagher –
VP, HR, Sue Ortenstone, John Sousa – VP, Communications and Community
Outreach, and Karen Yale - Director, Administrative Services.

Melody Meyer, representing Chevron, presented $18MM to Energy For Learning after hurricanes Katrina and Rita to rebuild the gulf coast schools.

66 Are you first quartile at what you do?" "If not, what is your plan to get there, and how can I help? **99**
—Lynn Laverty Elsenhans CEO and President, Sunoco, Inc. and Sunoco Logistics Partners LP

Chapter 6:
No Risk. No Reward

Taking risks at work can range from speaking up during a meeting to changing companies for career advancement. These are defining moments for your career. Risk taking is necessary for any woman who wants to move up in her organization.

Kathleen Eisbrenner, founder and CEO of her own company took risks. She earned a degree in civil engineering and served in various senior leadership positions with energy companies. At one point in her career, she and her leadership team left the national gas company where they were working to start a liquefied natural gas company. Eisbrenner became president of that company. After several years, she moved to a vice president LNG role with one of the five leading multinationals, allowing her to work as an ex-patriot. She has now moved into an entrepreneurial role.

Eisbrenner states that patience, courage, and the self-confidence to withstand the change process are important. Each change opens the door to new experiences. Take time to reflect on personal and professional performance, on your own or with a coach. Learning from past experiences as well as from those of others improves your ability to assess risk and increase your risk tolerance.

Step outside your comfort zone

The beginning of risk taking is stepping outside of your comfort zone. Earlier, we discussed the importance of lateral moves, nontraditional careers, and working at the next level as great ways to start taking risk early in your career. National relocations or expat assignments also challenge you outside of your comfort zone.

Every time you take a risk, you learn more about yourself and gain confidence. "Admit when you do not know something. It will make the risk much easier," says Peggy Montana of Shell Downstream, Inc. "Each time you take a risk, you build your confidence, and it is easier to take on the next challenging role."

Montana illustrated with a story. At one point in her career, she had an offer to move into Sales and Marketing. She was always in operations and this role was focused on customers, sales and pricing. She didn't have prior experience in this area of the business. The job was two levels up from where she was currently sitting, and was an outside role that was totally different from what she had been doing in her career. Montana turned down the opportunity at first, but then she decided to take the risk and accepted the opportunity to be considered for the job. In the end, she got the job.

> 66 Trust your instincts and take risks; focus on creating value, and money will follow. 99
> —Kathleen Eisbrenner, Founder and CEO, Next Decade, LLC

She learned quickly because she allowed the sales people to guide her, and she used the experience in the organization. She had great success in this role and says it was one she thoroughly enjoyed. The role refined her commercial skills, and she was able to hear first-hand feedback from the company's customers. She says, "Take risks, but admit it when you do not know something."

Like leadership, there is no "one-size-fits-all" solution in taking risk. Each woman has her own personality and ability to assume the responsibility and accountability that risk involves. Risk may happen on a daily basis, and some leaders embrace risk better than others. Young hires need to gain the confidence to step out of their comfort zone. Do not always depend on other people, even if you have great mentors; rather, take responsibility for managing your career.

Getting stakeholder buy-in before you present an idea lowers the risk of failure. Walk the floor of your department, and start discussing your ideas with others. Give them the opportunity to be a part of your vision. When possible, their feedback should be incorporated into your presentation, so that people feel that they are a part of what you are trying to accomplish.

Karyl McCurdy Lawson, of Phillips and Reiter, PLLC, is no stranger to risk taking. She changed the way that natural gas contracting was accomplished in the United States by initiating and leading the first model natural gas trading contract adopted by the predecessor of the North American Energy Standards Board (NAESB). Early in her career, she learned a lesson on risk taking when she took on a trailblazing topic that was controversial in the 1990s.

Calculated risk taking is an important element in leadership. Lawson brought this value to life when she decided to build workforce diversity into the organizational strategy of the natural gas company she previously worked for.

At that time, diversity was not even "on the radar" for energy companies, so Lawson took it upon herself to make a change. Her diversity program had remarkable results, and she gained great respect in the company. In nine months, the company went from one female officer to four and from zero African-American representation to two officers. The initiative opened the pipeline of officer-level talent among minorities.

If you are trailblazing a new area, Lawson recommends that you have a project charter and a champion from the senior management team. She stresses that it is critical to get buy-in from the top of the organization and support for your change effort; this makes it much easier to get support throughout the company. As you learn from others and build a safety net of people who know you and back you up, it is easier to make the next move.

Have the difficult conversations

There is a belief that "nice girls shouldn't fail at work." Managers identify high-potential females in the workplace and instead of challenging them with high-visibility projects or management assignments, they "protect them from failing" by keeping them in safe roles.

Women also sabotage their careers by not defending their role or speaking up when they see a change to their work assignments. Dr. Lois Frankel, author of *"Nice Girls Don't Get the Corner Office,"* writes that if you work nonstop without a break...worry about offending others and back down too easily, explain too much when asked for information, or 'poll' your friends and colleagues before making a decision, chances are you have been bypassed for promotions and ignored when you expressed your ideas. Although you may not be aware of it, girlish behaviors such as these are sabotaging your career! She continues to explain that if you recognize and change behaviors that say 'girl,' not 'woman,' the results will pay off in career opportunities you never thought possible—and in an image that identifies you as someone with the power and know-how to occupy the corner office.[10]

One of the women, who prefers not to be mentioned, was told in 1997 that a man would take her leading role in a project because he "had a family to support" even though he didn't have the knowledge or experience for the job. She was informed that her role would be to support, educate, and prop him up.

She had a family, too. She didn't accept this local directive and contacted a senior leader, the person responsible for managing the overall project on an international level. She gave him a brief on what she could do, what she would like to do, and where she had been effective in the organization.

[10] http://www.drloisfrankel.com/books_office.html.

This contact was successful, and she was ultimately deployed in a role that provided her greater satisfaction; in a different project. She recognized that prior to that phone call she had to consider what she would do if it didn't end well. Know what your "deal breakers" are, and be willing to leave if your conditions are not met.

Here is another story that ended well. Martha Wyrsch with Vestas-American Wind Technology, Inc. says that shortly after giving birth to her son, Peter (now twenty-two years old); she had been doing well in the firm and was on track to become a partner. All of a sudden, the deals she was being asked to handle changed and were not as challenging. She noticed that she was being treated differently than before. Wyrsch went to the partner who was in charge of her group for the energy practice and talked to him. He explained to her that they were sensitive to her being a mother and didn't want to overload her with challenging projects.

Perhaps the company's intentions were good, and the partners showed that they honored her new role as a mother. However, in a law firm, the only way to make partner is to work on challenging and fast-paced deals. Wyrsch explains that she had worked on such cases before giving birth, and she knew she could still do the same level of work.

In a private meeting, she thanked her boss and recognized that his heart was in the right place. She explained that what the partners were doing was jeopardizing her career and reputation, because her peers would think that she was no longer motivated and interested in making partner. It was important to address the issue with her boss. Wyrsch emphasized that she felt comfortable talking to him, because she knew her boss well, and they had worked on many deals together.

Too many times women sense a change of attitude but fail to address it immediately. Instead, we hope it will go away. You cannot be complacent or patient in raising issues when you see inequities. Perception is 99 percent of reality, and if you are being considered for an opportunity, not everyone is going to know you or your performance history. Take control of how you are perceived and the image you are creating.

Lynn Laverty Elsenhans, of Sunoco Logistics Partners LP, points out that early in her career she was offered roles that were in underperforming operations. At first, she viewed this as a safe role and opportunity. She turned this situation into a positive experience by taking these jobs and out-performing expectations. This became part of track record and was noticed by senior management.

She started to think more about how she could make a greater impact, based on the broad experience she developed in her previous assignments. She realized that she needed to express her concerns and ask for the more critical assignments she wanted and was ready for. She scheduled a meeting with senior management. After the conversation, it was not clear whether she would get a leadership role in a core area of operations for the company. She was certain that management heard her concerns but was not convinced they understood. It was the only time in her career that she thought she needed to start looking for another job.

Elsenhans says, "Understand that you need to be willing to have the conversations that sometimes make you feel uncomfortable, but you have to find a constructive way to have them. People cannot read your mind. You have to be willing to make a change to get what you want."

In the end, Elsenhans received a senior position. She became the vice president of refining in one of the largest integrated oil and gas companies in the world.

Balance the benefits with the risk

Sometimes you need to take risks. That may mean leaving your current company for the unknown. Changing companies can give you a big bump up the career ladder when the benefits outweigh the risk. The change should not be for a small advancement but rather a great improvement. It needs to be a conscious, considered choice.

Rebecca McDonald of Laurus Energy worked for ten different companies in her career, staying at one company for more than ten years. She recognized that some companies have good performance systems that move people along at the right pace, allowing for a great career path, while others do not.

> 66 Every day that we are blessed to be alive is an opportunity to learn something new. We should challenge ourselves and make the most of it! 99 —Cindy B. Taylor, President, Chief Executive Officer, and Director of Oil States International, Inc.

McDonald liked the feeling of being in charge; she knew she could do more and learn more, and sometimes the company she worked for held her back.

She learned not to ignore how she felt in her job. She understood what her strengths were and looked for roles with increasing responsibility that let her strengths guide her. If an opportunity did not add challenges or new skills, she discarded it. Money was not the driver, but promotions typically involved an increase in salary.

She never said she wanted to be a vice president. As she gained new skills and responsibilities in areas she enjoyed and excelled, it was natural for these roles to present themselves. Evaluate a job based on what you want to learn. McDonald notes, "Don't plan your career for your whole life. You will miss out on some incredible opportunities if you do. "

In her role as CEO for Laurus Energy, a Houston-based developer of underground coal gasification projects, McDonald did her due diligence on the technology. She respected the founders and embraced the idea of working in an entrepreneurial world.

Leverage your core competencies for change

Like a book, the chapters of your life and career should be able to stand alone but should all come together for a good ending. Taking your skill set to a new industry or company can be daunting, but it can provide new possibilities for a successful career.

As I was writing this book, Halina Caravello decided to leave Baker Hughes, an oilfield services company that provides services, tools and software, after twenty-three years. At the time she was their vice president of health, safety, environment and security. She wanted to move back to the East Coast, where she grew up, to be near her extended family. To make the move, she focused on skills that translated to a manufacturing company. She accepted a job as vice president for environment, health and safety with a highly diversified global manufacturer with their North American offices in her hometown of Princeton, NJ.

Caravello understood that her reputation, contacts, and relationships were in Houston and at her previous company. She admits that leaving these behind was the toughest part. She developed a good reputation and a personal brand that would not be known in a new company, and she would have to build her credibility and industry knowledge all over again.

She proves that a career in energy is portable and allows you to experience many different opportunities throughout your life. It teaches you management techniques uniquely tailored to the complexities of industry, as well as more generally appreciated leadership skills.

"Leading teams in critical projects, through economic downturns, and scenario planning are all skills you can take to another company or industry. If you plan well, being open and flexible, a career in energy will allow for many opportunities," Caravello says.

Laura Buss Sayavedra of Spectra Energy Partners, LP worked in government and international relations before moving into the energy industry. She came to the industry in the reverse process, with a completely different education and area of expertise. Her skills were highly valued, because she had international business and government experience that she could leverage with a company that was increasing its international activity.

She entered the industry when the natural gas sector was being reregulated. It was an advantage for her to not know the history of the industry, because she wasn't "set in her ways" with outdated paradigms. Sayavedra added value through her expertise in understanding how international infrastructure projects are financed and managed from a government relations/finance perspective.

Think about the transferable skills you have that can readily be leveraged into an industry position and what areas of a business will value those skills. Sayavedra states that the energy industry is changing dramatically, so new perspectives are highly valued in international business, renewables, social media, sustainability, and smart grid.

If you are interested in the energy sector, understand that there needs to be a balance between what you bring to a company and what you receive. If you are not in an "energy city," identify the links where you are: local energy distribution companies, energy technology companies, and government entities (both state and federal) that regulate the industry. Consider moving to one of the energy capitals like Calgary, Houston, and London.

Networking organizations can connect you to companies and people looking for talent. Meet with other professionals at the Women's Energy Network, business chambers, and professional organizations in energy cities to hear about opportunities. Use your university networks because someone in your alumni club may be employed in the industry. Present your "elevator speech" to a wide range of family and friends. Get their ideas, suggestions, and connections. Energy is a part of everything you do and use in your life. It is an exciting place to work.

66 So take advantage of opportunities and a little bit of luck as well.**99**
—Martha Carnes, Energy Assurance Partner, PricewaterhouseCoopers.

Chapter 7:
Choose your Lifestyle and Partner Wisely

Many young girls, especially those of the baby boomer generation, were raised on the Cinderella theory—our husbands would ride up on a beautiful white horse, wearing shining armor, and sweep us away to a wonderful life. Why do we take more time planning for college, a career, or even a vacation than we invest in the search for a compatible mate?

Lifestyle and partners were not my areas of focus for the interview, but I was surprised how many of the women mentioned the importance of choosing well and giving credit to their partners. Many realized that they would never have reached as far as they did without support at home. These women came from traditional families in which their mother didn't work or had a lesser career than their father. In the past men assumed that a woman would step aside for his career. The married women in the group I interviewed noted that now couples are finding ways to manage two aspiring careers. Their spouses took a more active role at home and from time to time, they even stepped back or worked from home.

They refer to their spouses as their "biggest fan," "supporter," "champion," "tag team spouse," "partner," and "life support." They advise women to be strategic about choosing their life partner and to discuss their careers prior to making a commitment.

Lynn Laverty Elsenhans and her husband made choices based on dual careers with no children. After the decision was made, their next choice was which city to live in. They chose Houston because they considered it a city that would be good for a dual-career couple and offer many companies to choose from. Even after all that thought and planning, Elsenhans was offered a job opportunity in Singapore and then London. Her husband gave up a CFO role to follow her.

I tell many young women that I mentor, "A very supportive partner makes the journey much easier and more fun. Then everything else will fall into place. If you get a white horse, it is a bonus."

Partners who scale back

Having a partner who is willing to take on a big role at home and is supportive of your career aspirations is more important than most people realize. For women, it is more of a challenge if there are children involved. Allowing your spouse to play a primary role in the house requires a different mindset. You must accept the fact that you cannot "do it all" and have to let some things go.

66 The most important choice that you will make in your life is who your life partner is; choose wisely. 99
— Lynn Laverty Elsenhans, Chief Executive Officer and President, Sunoco, Inc. and Sunoco Logistics Partners LP

Martha Wyrsch is president of her company's North American operations. She credited her husband, who scaled back on traveling to help more at home. When their eldest was starting high school, they decided that he would not work at all but would get involved with volunteer organizations, allowing him to be home during those critical teenage years.

Another woman who chose not to actively participate in my book due to work constraints shared a story with me that I want to include because I think it illustrates a good learning lesson about what really matters.

This woman realized that if she had stayed home, the standards would have been different. She found that her husband was able to instill a sense of independence in their child that she would not have been able to provide due to her desire to manage details. She remembered when her daughter was in a school celebration but due to meeting overload, she couldn't be at home to help her get ready. She arrived in time to see her young daughter on center stage in a mismatched outfit that only a five-year-old could select. She was mortified, but her unaware husband was proud of his beautiful daughter. At that moment, she realized that no one was harmed by the experience. In fact, her daughter was proud of the outfit she selected. Give up the things that truly are not important, that won't hurt anyone. Whether it is a perfect house or what you do for your child, choose wisely and according to the lifestyle you wish to live.

Gianna Manes of Duke Energy and her husband are a dual career couple. Her husband gave up traveling to be at home more with their two children. He goes to the office early while she has breakfast with their kids; he comes home to prepare dinner while she works late. Whether or not you decide to bring children into the equation, it is all about a partnership.

A supportive spouse can help you manage children while advancing in your career. Meg Gentle of Cheniere Energy became pregnant with her first son "a bit early in the time schedule," she laughs. She had already been accepted at Rice for her executive MBA program. She and her husband decided that she should start the program a week after giving birth and maintaining her full-time work schedule. Gentle realized that she would not have been able to pursue her career goals if her husband had not been supportive.

There has to be give and take. Sometimes the responsibilities are divided 60/40, with the other partner taking on more responsibility. There are many things that can detract your attention from your career, but these women chose supportive spouses who allowed them to shoot for the stars.

It is a balancing act

The women note that the lifestyle of the energy industry is not easy. It may include international travel, often to countries that are not exactly vacation spots. It is a 24/7 job that is critical to every aspect of our lives.

You are always balancing the time that you need to spend on the job and ensuring that the work gets done. You need to figure out how to spend time on the job, time with your family, and time for yourself.

Sometimes spouses take turns. Kathleen Hogenson, of Zone Energy, calls marriage a compromise. Hogenson married a geologist who had lived all over the world and was known for his discoveries. She and her husband took turns taking on new roles in new companies to accommodate each other's aspirations, working together for nineteen years.

Because both were trying to advance their careers, there was a point when Hogenson had to negotiate with her husband to leave his company because she got a better offer elsewhere. Her part of the bargain was that when his next job offer came along, she would move for him. His dream job was that of an exploration manager.

One year later, when her husband was offered an exploration manager position in Ecuador, they had a two-year-old daughter. At the time, Hogenson did not like the thought of moving to South America because they both would be working, and she was concerned her daughter would learn Spanish and not speak English. When I arrived for the interview, she told me her daughter, now twenty was in Pamplona, Spain, for the running of the bulls. She had just been in Barcelona watching Spain win the World Cup. Hogenson exclaims with great pride, "She speaks Spanish fluently and is having the time of her life!"

Not everything was perfect when they went to Ecuador. Her husband had his dream job, but she had to step back from a senior engineer position to engineer. However, within a year, Hogenson was the head of all reservoir completions and economics. At a very young age Hogenson led the team that managed a billion-dollar investment. Hogenson had the education, experience, and skill sets that made her valuable on a team where talent was not always available.

When they returned to the United States, many companies wanted to hire her because of her experience. The job launched her career, changed it completely, and altered her way of thinking, something she never anticipated when she moved for her husband's career.

Hogenson enjoyed the expat lifestyle. She believed she could work internationally without living overseas but that it would be more difficult. It requires a lot of travel and jet lag, "which may cause you to fall asleep when doing homework with your kids at night." She believes that you can understand the culture of the places you travel, but you cannot have a balanced work and family life when you are traveling all the time. "Being an expat allows a woman to have her cake and eat it too," she says.

Living overseas enables you to organize logistics much easier, especially when you live in a country that allows you to have a staff at home. "The kids are much more part of your social life in other cultures versus in the United States," she says. When overseas with her family, she felt balanced in a way that returned only when she started her own company. She recommends that every young woman should experience this lifestyle at least once in her career.

Susan Cunningham with Noble Energy and her husband have been able to maintain their dual-career-couple status while raising a family. Cunningham accepted an expat position with a previous company when she was six months pregnant. Her company asked her to lead an operational office in Copenhagen for two years. She and her husband talked about the transition. He was working in a consulting company with clients in Europe, so it was easy for him to move and maintain some of his client base.

They worried about moving their newborn overseas, but they were able to take a friend's high school-aged daughter with them to help them adjust in their new home until they found a local nanny. "It's not always easy to find the right answer, but if you remain determined that you are going to find a way, you will, and that's exactly what we did," confirms Cunningham.

International careers for dual-career couples

Some women choose an expat assignment as part of their career path.
They realize that personal flexibility with a partner and family is essential
to take advantage of these opportunities. From a career standpoint,
working in multiple locations in a variety of leadership roles, particularly
internationally, is excellent for developing global business leadership.

Elsenhans stresses that a senior person in a truly global company will
need to do at least one assignment outside of the United States. Suzanne
Nimocks traveled a lot in her career but never lived overseas. In hindsight,
she wishes she had lived in Asia or Latin America. It is her belief that living
abroad always adds value to the leadership experience.

Melody Meyer, with Chevron, worked rotational schedules in Angola and
Kazakhstan early in her career and recommends this lifestyle if you can
create flexibility at home. She explains, "To be a leader in this industry, you
have to have deep experience in a variety of countries, venues, fiscal terms,
and governments. You must participate in some start-ups as well as mature
operations, offshore, onshore and everything else." She believes that some
people can have a fulfilling career being in one location, but it does not
prepare you as well as international relocations. Meyer understands that it
is not always possible for everybody to travel or live overseas and that not
everyone wants that. She recommends that you be honest with what you
want and develop your career plan and experiences based on your decision.

Meyer's success was built on the flexibility to move for her work and
taking on nontraditional roles. She has been a change agent, creating
value and improved performance wherever she has worked. If her spouse
did not support her career ambitions, she probably would still have been
successful in her company, but it would have been different. "A supportive
spouse makes the journey better," she says.

She found a creative way to balance her life while working a 28/28 rotation
in Kazakhstan and Angola for almost eight years. At that time, she was part

of a dual-career couple with three children that were three, six, and eight. She missed every other Christmas, national holiday, and sometimes birthdays, and people tried to figure out how she and her husband did it. "The key to it was an excellent network, organization, and personal flexibility," she says.

Alternative schedules and extensive travel, even with children at home, is possible. It took creativity and advance planning and required that the time at home was of maximum quality. For example, during her twenty-eight days off, she created a "28/28 Girl Scout troop" where she was the leader when she was home and another mom led when she was gone for twenty-eight days. She had a great home network that was willing to be flexible and to help.

She explains that she was able to volunteer at the preschool when she was on her home rotation for almost a month, which she couldn't have done working a 5/2 schedule. When she missed birthdays, a special event, or a holiday, she prepared presents, decorations and even the logistics of parties before she left in order to make it special while she was away. The family celebrated again when she returned. She wanted to make sure that she was not an "absentee mom."

Her children adapted, and they talked about life in terms of hitches. Meyer and her family saw the rotation schedule as opportunities to travel and create a fun schedule of activities that would normally not be possible if she were in an office or at a local site. She recommends the schedule when all the right support systems are in place. It provides an opportunity to fully immerse yourself in your work and to fully immerse yourself in family during that period.

The career development opportunity by working in the more challenging international operating environments far outweighed the rotational challenges.

Meyer and her family traveled internationally, but they never lived together outside of the United States. She explains that her mother never worked outside the home, and her father held the traditional role in the household. Many of the women I interviewed come from a generation that would not ask their husband to give up his career for theirs. In hindsight, many wish they had considered it.

America's workforce has undergone immense change over the past forty years, bringing with it societal changes that impact the way people view traditional family roles and dual-career compromises. Meyer and her husband are part of that change. Her husband eventually quit working to support her career and to care for their three teenage children. He takes on leadership roles at school and the community.

Meyer was recently promoted to her new role as president of Chevron Asia-Pacific Exploration and Production Company and has moved to her company's headquarters in San Ramon, California, with an office in Singapore. When I met with her shortly after the announcement, I asked her if she would like to experience expat life now. She smiles and says, "Anything is possible." I believe her.

Not all of us are married when we take on expat assignments. I actually met my Dutch husband when I was living in Brazil for a previous company. Barbara Heim of BG Group states that an international career as a single can be fun but stressful. She remembers when she took an expat assignment in Switzerland and didn't have the built-in companionship that couples have. She threw herself into work 24/7 and almost missed a wonderful opportunity to get to know the local culture. After a time, she looked around and started to connect with others. "In the beginning, you think it is the job and the content, but it is also about the people," she says.

Two homes, two countries

Traditional marriage still exists. People meet, fall in love, and marry, but with the Internet and a 24/7 work style, relationships today are different from when our parents tied the knot. In 2005, according to The Center for the Study of Long-Distance Relationships (LDR), an estimated 2.9 percent of marriages in the United States were considered "long distance," and one in ten marriages included a period at distance within the first three years. This means that in 2005, approximately 3,500,000 people in the United States alone were involved in long-distance marriages.[11]

When my husband received a promotion for a role that was based out of The Netherlands, we decided that I would stay in Houston. Our thought was to give it one year and see what happened. It is important to set expectations or a limit of how long you want to live in a long-distance situation.

According to the articles from the Center for LDR, it appears we did most things correctly. I am not going to say it was easy, but because his role was global and my company was based out of northwest Europe, it was possible to manage within our professional travel. The longest time we spent apart was seven weeks, but with the Internet, video cameras, and phone calls, we were able to still be a part of each other's lives and decision making. This lifestyle takes some of the spontaneity out of life, but for two people who love to plan, this played to our strengths.

The Center for LDR claims that long-distance relationships are successful when couples live in the same place for a period of time to get to know each other and build trust. The key is compatibility, not proximity. The frequency of breakups in long-distance relationships is not greater than that of relationships where partners are close to one another, suggesting that our needs from romantic relationships are more emotional and psychological than physical.[12]

It is never too late to take the plunge if you want that one-year expat assignment. It is possible that your partner will not or cannot go with you for work or other reasons. If your partner is taking the overseas experience, do not feel that you are being left behind. Separation can make the heart grow fonder, and it will allow time for areas of interest that your partner may not enjoy.

[11] http://www.waiit.com/Long_Distance_Relationships_Statistics, March 5, 2011.
[12] http://www.waiit.com/Long_Distance_Relationships_Statistics, March 5, 2011.

If you are being relocated and your spouse wants to go with you, he could ask for a sabbatical, if you can afford it. I left a company for the opportunity to explore Argentina with my husband. I took a job with an American company, wanting to expand its presence in South America. It wasn't the perfect job, but it allowed me to maintain my foothold in the energy industry.

❝ Your life is important, so make a good decision, and do not give up something you will regret later. **❞**
—Cheryl Collarini, owner of Collarini Energy Staffing, founder of Collarini Engineering and Etroa Resources, an E&P Company.

There will always be work but not always opportunities to discover new destinations with your partner. There are few excuses not to go, and grow, in new places together.

Tradeoffs for advancement

The number of American women without children has risen to an all-time high of one in five (a jump from the 1970s when one in ten women ended their childbearing years without having a baby, according to the Pew Research Center).[13]

Part of the reason for the rise in the number of childless women is an overall pattern toward delaying marriage and having children, the research showed. The increase in career opportunities is one of the trends that led to the change in statistics for women over forty.

Barbara Heim is vice president for human resources for her company. She intentionally did not marry; she wanted the flexibility to move with her career and not worry about disrupting other people's lives. She made more than seventeen physical moves in her career and could not have imagined

[13] http://pewresearch.org/pubs/1642/more-women-without-children April 30, 2011.

it with a family. It is not a lifestyle she wants forever, but it was her choice early on.

Samina Farid, is Chairman of her own company. She started her company thinking that it would be perfect to raise kids while working from a home office. She soon realized it was a crazy idea. For Farid, it was eat-sleep-work and nothing else for the first few years, and it never felt like the right time to have children. It took a lot of sacrifice to launch a company, and her company brings her great satisfaction. She is proud of the reputation her company has built globally and enjoys mentoring younger employees and watching them grow and succeed.

Not everyone is willing to move or has the flexibility to do so. Cheryl Collarini, an oil and gas entrepreneur was working for an international oil company and realized that moving would be part of her next promotion. She worked for a company based in Houston, lived in New Orleans with her husband and children, and was close to her extended family. Due to some sad circumstances, she did not want to move away from her parents. She knew that she would be overlooked in the company if she did not move so in 1985 – the worst time for the industry – she started her own company.

Collarini knew that it is not easy having your own business. People often have the illusion that self-employment is easy and life is better if you have your own company and are your own boss. She explains that as a consultant, she billed by the hour. A normal month for someone working for a large company is about 170 hours, and a normal month for her was 300 hours. She was selling her technical services during the day and billing her hours doing the work at night.

If you want to start your own business, she advises the following. Get a good accountant and a lawyer who is not a part-time travel agent. (She admits that she initially tried to go cheap on the accounting and legal issues, but because she had an MBA, it was easier to oversee the accounting.) Collarini remembers that it was a life-changing experience to have her own business after working in a multinational company that had all the services like IT, accounting and purchasing readily available.

"Make your business or career work around your life. Everyone finds a way that is personal. Make a decision early on how you want to do it," she says.

Chapter 8:
Career or Family

There is ample proof that women are capable of holding senior management positions in energy companies, so what obstacles prevent women from getting through the talent pipeline? All 31 women I interviewed talked about work/life balance. Depending on your age and where you are in your career you may not be experiencing the following issues of balancing your career and home life; with or without children. However, it is an important chapter to read so that you can understand the conflict that many of your peers or bosses are dealing with day-to-day.

One thing that all the women want to make clear is presented by Martha Carnes of PwC. "Don't make assumptions that because you are a woman and you have a family that there will be career limitations, because you are probably placing them on yourself without reason."

The women I interviewed mentioned that work/life balance is the number one obstacle for high potential talent at work. The decisions that young women make relating to career and family can often derail their journey up the corporate ladder or force them to miss out on an important aspect of life that they later regret.

Cheryl Chartier of Foster Wheeler is part of a dual-career couple with three children. She and her husband take turns balancing their workload and travel, and both try to maintain some flexibility for the other's career.

"Do not give up the idea of having a career and children, and do not worry about trying to be superwoman either. Trust me, we all get our capes caught in the door every now and then," says Chartier. She advises women that timing and balance are "never perfect."

In a society filled with conflicting responsibilities and commitments, work/life balance is an important topic. The women I interviewed discussed how they managed high-level careers and childcare without giving up what they wanted most in their lives: a life to go home to. You are not alone in this challenge, nor are you the first person to feel the weight of imbalance.

Compartmentalize your life

According to one school of thought, work/life balance is a choice. It is a broad concept including proper prioritizing between work and life. Ronald Claiborne writes, "Life is the result of all actions taken by choice over the course of time while fulfilling one's purpose in life. Therefore it is essential that we find a balance to fulfill our professional ambitions and happiness at home."[14]

A more recent group frames work/life balance as less of a zero sum choice. Julie Morgenstern proposes a new definition: "Work/life balance is not about the amount of time you spend working versus not working. It's more about how you spend your time working and relaxing, recognizing that what you do in one fuels your energy for the other."[15]

Mayor Annise Parker notes that the idea of work/life balance implies some evenness between work and home. She says that in real life, one part of your life or the other takes precedence. Sometimes the job overwhelms everything, and then there are days when home life is critical. Parker found that in her current role as Mayor of Houston, work definitely overwhelms her life commitments. She says that you have to understand when it is important to focus on home and set the job aside. She and her life partner adopted young children who are now fifteen, nineteen, and thirty-four years old. Her children know that if they need her she is there, but they also understand that the nature of her job is intense.

[14] http://www.helium.com/items/1519684-a-definition-of-work-life-balance, October 1, 2010.
[15] http://www.businessweek.com/business_at_work/time_management/archives/2008/07/work-life_balan.html.

It is about taking decisions, compartmentalizing your life, making sure you get the job done, and knowing when to say "enough for today" and relax. The women I interviewed warned that if you want a high-potential career and not a nine-to-five job, you have to be proactive and develop some good habits. With or without children, it is critical to set up a solid life infrastructure that allows you the freedom to do what you need to do— freedom not to worry about your home or that your child is the last one picked up from school because a parent is running late.

Laura Buss Sayavedra, vice president and CFO for her company says, "Women do not need to feel that it is necessary to choose between their career and family if they are interested in combining both of them." As a senior executive and a mother, she cautions that there are tradeoffs, and many times you cannot do everything you want every day.

Sayavedra remembered when she was offered a job that was a solid step to advancement for her career, and it was during the years that she gave birth to her two children. When her children were toddlers, she received her first vice president role. She found that taking on the role is possible, but it takes the development of your life infrastructure and support team.

Ask yourself "what is really important today," as this will change over time. "Delegating and outsourcing" are the words I heard for cleaning and cooking. Sayavedra remembers that when she had two young children, her work/life balance was stressful. Her small family was overwhelmed with laundry, and she tried to figure out what her support system should be (nanny, daycare, housekeeper). Because the young couple could not hire a housekeeper or nanny at that time, she outsourced the laundry to the neighborhood "washateria" and was able to maintain a sane, clean household.

I learned in the conversations about the importance of setting clear expectations and understanding that work/life balance is a challenge that you have to continually work on. Living in the present is most important. Meg Gentle, with Cheniere Energy, views her family time as an appointment on her calendar. "It is the most important appointment in my day, and it is not okay to miss it."

Gentle learned about disciplined time management from a boss she had prior to her dual-career marriage with five children. Her boss was completely committed to the job, but he had an end to the day when he went home to his wife and soccer team—his non-work life. She was on the team that he managed. Initially, his team did not leave when he did but watched him go live his life. After a while, they realized that it was important to have a balance and that the job is not always the highest priority.

When she started leaving at five or six o'clock, she realized that "you fill the time you give yourself to finish something." She left meetings that extended into the evening, telling the staff that she had "an appointment" to go to. Her appointment was dinner at home and putting the children to bed. Gentle stressed the importance of eating dinner as a family, and whatever happened at work between 6:00 and 9:00 p.m., she picked up after everyone in the house was asleep. She is known to send email at 2:00 am; this worked well for her because the house was quiet and she could focus.

Gianna Manes is the senior vice president and chief customer officer for her company. She says, "I am not always there, but I try to be there for the important things in life. I try to engage my children and make a point of keeping them involved. From time to time, I bring them to my office, so they understand where I go and a little of what I do."

Peggy Montana is an executive vice president for her company. She remembered the challenges this kind of job can have with a family. Her children were young when the demands of her career were greatest. She was responsible for health, safety and environment, foremen and union staff, production, budgets, and more. If there was a fire or another crisis in the refinery, she had to be there. She remembered calling home to say that she did not know when she would leave work and the nanny would have to stay until her husband arrived. One time when she was traveling, her husband had a crisis at work. That was when your life infrastructure plays a critical role.

Montana advises young women, "Do not obsess over the money. If you have dual careers, use the income to have the peace of mind that your kids are safe and well cared for." She advises to "make sure you always have plan B if plan A implodes" and that it does get easier over time. Kids grow up and become self-sufficient, and the demands decrease. As a senior manager, she is still "plugged in 24/7" but has more flexibility.

For many women, "plan B" includes grandparents and extended family that come to the rescue. Whether sending the children for a visit or importing grandparents, back-up plans were recurring themes.

Paula Harris, with Schlumberger, had just given birth and was required to travel to Australia for one month. She called her mother-in-law and asked if she wanted to babysit. On her flight to Perth, she flew from Houston to Chicago and left her baby in the care of a very happy grandmother.

> 66 Do not expect every day to be in balance; try to achieve balance overall. Have other interests and a life outside of work. 99
> —Gianna Manes, Senior Vice President and Chief Customer Officer for Duke Energy Corporation

Some say that having support to raise your family compromises half of the work/life equation and waters down the experience of parenting. Women have the majority of the burden and typically are the ones who take time off after birth. If you are a single mother or half of a dual-career couple with children, no one will deny that the balance changes and the decisions you have to make increase. It is a delicate balance between making sure that your children are well cared for and making sure that you have room to grow in your career. There are times you cannot have it all. Sometimes you will feel that you are doing so many things that you are not good at anything. There are days when life is unbalanced. It is all about

juggling your priorities and knowing that you will have some
responsibilities that you cannot drop. Whether they are at work that
day or at home that day, keep them all moving and make sure that you
have help.

Karyl McCurdy Lawson heads the energy practice at Phillips and Reiter,
PLLC. When she was a recently divorced mom, her boss at a natural
gas utility asked if she would move to Washington, DC to participate in
the Congressional Assistant Program. It was a great opportunity that would
entail unpredictable hours and evening events. It was a difficult period with
respect to balancing her professional and personal life with a five-year-old
son and living in a new city with no support system. Traditional childcare
or an hourly nanny would not work for her.

Although she did not want to give up her privacy, Lawson decided to have
a live-in au pair so that she wouldn't have to worry about the well-being
of her son. This proved to be a great decision, and she continued to have
live-in nannies until her son was twelve.

She relates a funny story about her first au pair that was a pretty, twenty-
one-year-old blonde from Sweden. Lawson recalls that men were instantly
attracted to her. One day, when Lawson answered the doorbell, a young
man looked surprised to see her and asked, "Could I see the attractive
younger blonde who lives here?"

Most of the women I spoke with had a nanny, and some were lucky to have
the same nanny over the course of their children's younger lives. Whether
they were live ins or hourly workers, they kept the lives of these women
and their families together.

Ask for support

Sue Payne with ExxonMobil Exploration Company found that one of the
biggest stressors young women have today is asking the company to
adjust or help them with their personal circumstances. They are afraid

to ask because of how it might "make them look" and that it would affect their next promotion. She claimed that she never felt negativity about women in the workforce and certainly never because they occasionally brought their babies to work or needed someone to take care of their family. Bringing her daughter to the office was a rare occurrence. Being a woman adds unique challenges when working full time, and if you are a single mother, it can be even more challenging, but there are many who have decided to do it (and are still doing it) and make it work.

Payne remembered when she went to work in a role that was demanding and she was always on call. She hired a full-time student at George Mason University, and they worked out their schedules and logistics to make sure that her daughter was always cared for. She recalled that there were times when even the best plan imploded and improvisation saved the day. Payne called plan B "managing in the moment."

She remembered a particular Sunday night when she got a call from one of her colleagues who did the "well report" for all the executives every Monday morning. He called her from the airport, stating that he had to go overseas and she had to cover for him in the morning meeting. It was the week her nanny was on vacation.

On Monday, she took her daughter to work early in the morning. Her daughter was relaxed about being at the office, because she had been there on many Sundays. Some of the men who would be in the meeting had children and did not want her daughter left alone in an office, waiting for her mom. That morning, Payne gave the well report with her four-year-old in the room, and everyone understood. The president even invited her daughter back because he understood that for Payne to do her job, the company would have to make accommodations from time to time.

When her daughter was a teenager, she requested flexibility and limited travel, because her parenting was really needed. During critical times, families must make sure that their children are surrounded by guidance and support. Payne has been with her company over thirty years and has raised her daughter through it all.

Martha Wyrsch, with Vestas-American Wind Technology, Inc., strongly recommends not being embarrassed or shy about the fact that you are a mother and have other things going on in your life. She says, "You have to keep that balance and, in fact, others respect it when you do."

Wyrsch recalled a difficult business transaction that required a lot of negotiation and late nights. She was in San Francisco and her family was in Charlotte, NC. Her daughter was young, and in the middle of a meeting, Wyrsch asked to step out of the conference room to say goodnight to her. She sang to her daughter every night, and as she was singing, one of the executives from the other company walked into the hallway but quickly left, realizing that he had intruded. Afterward, he commented that it was then that he turned the corner in the negotiation. He realized that while they were trying to settle a serious problem, she took the time to care for her family. The negotiations were successful, and now the executive and Wyrsch are friends. He continues to remind her of that night when her tune changed everything.

All the women I spoke with agreed that you need to ask for support when it is necessary, whether for your children, aging parents, or a sick family member. The women recommend that when asking for support, focus on stating what you want. Be direct when you make a request. Don't leave it to the listener to figure out what you want, and don't ignore the situation, hoping that it will get better. If it is a new request for your boss or company, ask for a trial solution to see how it works, and allow your team to get used to the new arrangement.

Here is an example of a family decision that could have stalled or ended a fabulous career. Instead, it had a positive affect for many mothers due to a compassionate and creative boss.

Cheryl Chartier, vice president for marketing and proposals at her company, remembers the challenges she faced as a working mom. After giving birth to her first son, she thought that daycare would be the answer, but her child got sick. The ordeal was a nightmare for a first-time mother. She thought she would have to quit her job or go part-time.

She had an understanding boss who asked questions and prevented her from quitting or going part time. He adjusted her schedule, allowing her to work thirty hours from the office and ten hours from home each week while she adjusted to her new life. He was supportive, saw value in her, and did not want to let her go.

There was no corporate policy in place at the time for such a decision, so Chartier and her boss were blazing new ground. She agreed to try this arrangement for three months and then review it, but it ended up lasting a year, because she was more productive with the flexibility of this arrangement. When she was in the office, she designated hours for her team members to come in for guidance and questions, and then there was plenty of time for her to do paperwork at home.

She asked for additional support in the form of a "mother's room" so that other new mothers in her organization could have a private place for nursing. The company organized a conference room, complete with the pumps and nursing kits, as well as a refrigerator. The room was kept locked, and each mother had a key. It was included on the conference room reservation system so that they could plan their days accordingly. This was an inexpensive solution that showed that the women were valuable employees. It was all about asking for what they needed, and the solution improved the company's reputation.

Chartier is involved in groups like WEN, because she understands that all women need help from time to time. She says that young women wonder if working and having a family is possible. She encourages them to hang in there and look for support. She sees too many young women who start a fabulous career but give it all up when they have children because they think there is no other alternative.

Rebecca McDonald of Laurus Energy states, "If a company does not understand or value what you are doing, change companies. Do not let a company limit your life and take you away from something that you want to do. A company that really values you will never put you in a position to give up a lifestyle choice. If you really believe they will not promote you because of a life-balance decision, you should challenge it, and if it is true, look elsewhere. It is important that you take a personal stance and let your boss and company know."

Part of asking for support is having the courage to not miss the important things in your life. McDonald remembered when she was working for a major oil and gas company, and her son was graduating. It was something she wouldn't miss for the world. However, on that same day, her chairman of the company wanted her to speak at a worldwide leadership conference. This was a big deal for the company and global community, because she would be the first woman to present for the company. She called the chairman, told him that she couldn't do it, and asked him to support her role as a mother.

Her chairman was stunned and disappointed at first, but he realized that she had made a lot of compromises for the company and this was one compromise she would not make. McDonald set her boundary, and he understood that they needed to find a solution. They agreed to videotape her speech in advance.

Both men and women at the conference were surprised at the flexibility the company provided her, as that was not the norm. In the end, both were winners. The chairman received better press than he ever expected by showing the entire organization that family comes first.

McDonald notes that it is not easy, and the situation could have gone in another direction. She adds that, luckily, she was not faced with too many of these decisions. She acknowledges that you have to decide what you are willing to give up and know the implications. There is a balance that works for every woman, and that woman has to find it.

You can have it all, just not all at once

When trying to find balance, most of us readily agree that a career, a family, and international travel cannot fit neatly into a forty-hour week. The question is how to prioritize choices.

Lynn Laverty Elsenhans, with Sunoco Logistics Partners LP, explains that she had strict boundaries around work/life balance. People may not believe it, but when she went home, she left her work behind. There were times when she worked twelve to fourteen hours a day because a particular job was that important for the company and her development. She understood at that moment that she needed to dedicate time to get through that job, but she also realized that she was not willing to do so every day for her entire career.

Before Elsenhans and her husband married, they talked about whether or not to have children and decided that they would not. That decision made their work/life balance and dual careers easier.

The women I interviewed recognized that the generations have changed, and younger people probably value their free time more. The baby boomer generation saw a time of transition. Women fought hard for their roles in the workplace, and often that meant sacrifices and long hours. Unfortunately, still today, it is difficult to reach a senior management position within a matter of years if you are not willing to put some extra effort into the job. Getting to "the top" requires effort and time. This is true in sports and the arts, and the business world is the same.

It requires setting boundaries and making adjustments to make it work, and sometimes it requires giving up something you truly enjoy. However, those changes do not have to be forever, and they can have positive effects. After giving birth to her son, Meg Gentle who is now senior vice president and CFO for her company began to migrate away from international commercial roles and into financial roles with less travel. She changed companies to avoid a long commute that kept her away from home. It is important to find a balance that works for you and allows you to grow in your company.

Her changes did not limit her career as she moved up in her organization to her current role. "There is a richness of life that seems to be missing without continual exposure to new places and different cultures, but it is more than compensated with a different kind of richness that comes from spending the time with my two small children, three grown stepchildren, and one beautiful granddaughter," Gentle says. She has confidence that eventually life will have room for the international part that she loves. She reminds women that they should not be afraid to ask for flexibility.

66 It has been the most important thing to me, being able to live a life that is bigger than just my work. 99
—Meg Gentle, Senior Vice President and CFO, Cheniere Energy

Sharon Michael Owens with Centerpoint Energy remembers when she was starting her career over thirty years ago when there were few women in the company. The workforce competed to see who the last person was to leave the office. She notes that the company attitude changed as more women worked there. Even the men realized they should be home watching their children's sports games. While the "how many hours did you work today" culture persists in many companies, most employers are more aware of the decisions that people make to raise children and have a life outside of work. Technology helps too.

Barbara Heim, with BG Group, Americas and Global LNG, states, "I happen to subscribe to the theory that work/life balance is a very personal thing." Heim appreciated it when her boss noticed that she was working hard on an exciting project that energized her more than going home at five o'clock. She understands that other women may complain that they have no work/life balance, but she also realizes it is easier for her because she is single with no children.

She tells young executives that there are many roles to choose from and some of those are highly visible in the company that typically does not fit conveniently into a forty-hour week. She says that many times those roles include a lot of travel, long hours, and evening commitments. If you have a set of candidates where some are willing to put in the time and effort and others are more rigid, it is easy to predict who is going to get the more-demanding jobs.

Heim recognizes that there are different demands on people. Some are more rigid due to family requirements while others do not have the desire and ambition to work beyond their eight hours. Her company takes this information into consideration when promoting candidates.

She says, "If you are happy with your life and love the fact that you do not have to travel and you can leave at five, that's fine. There is nothing wrong with that; we need people who are willing to be stability players. Stability players usually do not get the rewards like those willing to go the extra mile. Be realistic and don't complain that you if didn't reach the C-suite, blaming it on your work/life decisions. Balance is just that: balance."

Look for work options that promote balance

The women I interviewed made it clear that work/life balance in the energy industry does not mean an equal balance. As a leader, you will need to strive for evenness for you and your team, and having a clear understanding of when your skills are required for the task at hand. The willingness to put in the effort is critical for your success. There will be irregular hours. Learning how to work effectively and knowing when it is time to go home will provide a sense of balance. Be aware of the companies that require you to work eighty hours irrespective of the workload; this is not necessary or healthy.

Recently, a leading multinational oil company was surprised to learn that a majority of its high-potential females were single income households or had spouses that were managing their careers from the home. This showed that the environment for talent was changing, as well as the balance at home.

Understand that sometimes companies do not know what is going on in your personal life. It is your manager's responsibility to support your career ambitions, and it is your responsibility to manage your career and work/life balance decisions. You need to determine what is acceptable and what is not.

Cheryl Chartier of Foster Wheeler had great success establishing work/life balance with a previous boss. However, she did have an experience later on in a different company that required her to set the boundaries of what was acceptable. She was offered a foreign assignment on a single status. At that time, she had a two-year-old and a four-month-old at home. She was asked to move to Australia. Chartier told the company that her family had to come with her, and the company had to provide employment for her husband who was not going to give up his career. The company agreed.

Part of the move included Chartier signing a medical release document that stated, "You do not intend to get pregnant while on assignment." Having two small children already, her immediate plan was not a third child, at least not for a while. Two months into the assignment, she became pregnant. She shared this experience to highlight that these types of policies are not acceptable.

Today, companies may not be asking you to sign a medical release document, but they may be asking you to give up a life/balance choice that is important to you. Rebecca McDonald stated earlier that you must decide for yourself what is important, take a stance and let your boss know. Understand the consequences of your choices, noted Barbara Heim.

There is much talk about bridging roles with part-time work or work sharing. These arrangements would help everyone, and not just women, through childrearing or elderly parent care. Companies should develop these programs if they are going to balance short-term aspects with long-term gain. Companies need to encourage senior staff to partake in the flexible programs. They will be the role models young women need to see when they are making decisions based on career or family.

"If women had more options and weren't afraid to exercise them, we wouldn't lose the talent and investment," claims Peggy Montana of Shell Downstream, Inc. Women of all ages may think that using flexible programs will be detrimental to their careers; they might not be taken seriously or not be perceived as a "hard worker." Corporate leaders need to understand that presence in the office does not necessarily drive performance.

If flexibility is important to you, seek out companies that already offer such programs or spearhead new options in your organization. There are companies that have programs for working moms who need additional support and resources to fulfill their career ambitions. There are also companies that are developing programs for their working mothers. Make a decision early on which company provides the ideal work arrangement for the lifestyle you want.

Martha Carnes leads the energy practice for her company. She mentions that they are piloting a program that is customized to the individual woman's needs (they offer it to men, too). The firm has three-month sabbaticals. "We believe it's critical to have your personal life in order, enabling you to perform your best at work," she states.

At PwC, an employee can leave the firm for up to five years. The employee needs to participate in all of the training programs that help keep them connected with the firm and come back within five years. Women sometimes need to be home with their children or take care of elderly parents, and PwC accommodates its high-performing talent in these areas.

The big four accounting firms have made changes and are successfully retaining female talent and promoting women. Energy companies have long since accepted that talented women are a highly desirable segment of the work force. As women continue to outnumber men in the ranks of college graduates, that acceptance will only increase. The flexible programs that exist today are typically used by the administrative staff with no executive role models. As more and more women enter the energy industry, this will change.

It is not perfect. In the energy industry, glaring problems and pockets of resistance against accommodating a different work style still exist. We cannot deny that the "old guard" still upholds barriers that prevent women from breaking the glass ceiling. It is not just work arrangements that women struggle with, but a cultural inflexibility. Some companies think they are doing what is necessary, but in reality, they "just don't get it."

In a recent series on women in the workforce, The Economist reported that motherhood is the largest obstacle to women advancing in the corporate world (not just the energy industry): "Motherhood, not sexism, is the issue: in America, childless women earn almost as much as men, but mothers earn significantly less."[16] If we are to become a workplace that reflects American values of fairness and equality, we still have some changes to make in how we view family and work. Organizations that embrace those values will do better, because they will attract and retain the best talent.

Barbara Lavery, executive coach challenges women to get their voice heard. Determine what would improve the culture of the energy industry as a whole and then specifically for your company or niche. She says that there are fears, expectations, and ideas behind the barriers that prevent women from advancing in their careers. It is important to understand these issues before you try to change your company's culture toward women. The voice of female leaders is critical to design programs that allow companies to meet current talent needs and to build a female talent pipeline. Internal women's groups might develop a charter for cultural improvement. Which of these groups are successful? Learn from those who have gone before you and achieved success, and know that doing it alone won't work.

---

[16] http://www.economist.com/node/15174489, March 26, 2011.

"There are allies in the leadership team, willing to partner with you and address the barriers, "Lavery says. "Get them involved. Be wary of those who know what words to say but are not emotionally attached to the idea of change."

In recent years, considerable resources have been spent on recruiting and developing women and minority employees. The generations are different in the way they value free time, and the way people work has changed. The energy industry will need to develop work arrangements and test them within their ranks to attract and retain young female talent. (This would be valuable for young men as well.)

66 Balance between life and work exists; it just doesn't happen on the same day. 99 —Joan Eischen, Author, *Energy and the City* and Director, Advisory at KPMG, LLP, Houston

Chapter 9:
Make the Move to Energy and the City

I trust from the stories and the career advice that was given, you will join us in the energy industry. Energy is a multidisciplinary field that provides limitless opportunities. The technical women I interviewed recommend the STEM disciplines, but there are a wide range of career options for other degrees; although technical affinity is an advantage.

Determine the kinds of experiences you want to have; travel, technology, management, finance or legal to name a few. Is the oil and gas industry for you or would you prefer working in the development of alternative energy such as wind, biodiesel or solar? In alternative energy, for example, there are opportunities in policy making that do not require a deep technical background. Understanding finance, development, and the environment can increase your competitiveness. Knowing specific regions and languages can also provide marketable skills.

> 66 You want a career that will consume you and totally engages you; work that is so fascinating that it stretches you beyond belief. 99
> —Rebecca McDonald, CEO of Laurus Energy

There is a pipeline for talent for men and women, but the three topics that I presented in this book seem to be the filters that keep women from reaching senior leadership in a male dominant industry. The women I interviewed experienced or see their young employees struggle with these three areas: visibility, sponsors and work/life balance.

The greatest is work/life balance. It can be done if you develop a strong infrastructure and always have a plan B. If you are a recent graduate, chances are you are young and single and not worrying about spouses and childcare. Heed the warning from the women I interviewed: Choose your lifestyle and partner wisely.

The other area to focus on is the development of your brand; one that will make you visible in a bastion of maleness. It is easy to be noticed as the "only girl in the room," but understand why they are noticing you. Is your attire appropriate, are you communicating effectively, are you being heard when you make a decision?

Without a sponsor you may break the glass ceiling, but it will take longer. I recently spoke with a woman who was just promoted to a senior executive position. She explained to me that she and her mentor prepared a three year plan for development to allow her the opportunity to ask her senior leadership team for the role. I couldn't help thinking, "A sponsor would have gotten her there faster." We do not want to discourage mentoring, because it is important in your development, but a sponsor is required for advancement.

As women continue to join the ranks of employees in the energy industry, these obstacles will disappear. The women I interviewed, and many more, are helping break down these barriers. Although women's work is as varied as the women themselves, they are taking on non-traditional roles and proving that it is not gender that should define a role, but competence.

For young professionals, Houston is a great place to start a career. It has always been a city for visionaries, men and women who aren't afraid to take chances, who aren't afraid to push boundaries, and who understand that you're either moving forward or you're falling behind. It all started back at Spindletop: the first great oil discovery in Texas.

Houston is the best city to live, work, and play, according to Kiplinger's Personal Finance. It was named the best city to buy a home and the best U.S. city to earn a living by Forbes magazine. For those who want to make a difference and work hard, Houston offers a lot of opportunity, and the city continues to grow and add jobs. As Jeff Moseley, president and CEO of the

Greater Houston Partnership points out, "Houston is known for energy but it is also home to the largest concentration of medical professionals in the history of the world. Don't forget that "Houston" was the first word spoken from the moon and is home to NASA. It is an international city with the kindest, warmest and most charitable people you will ever meet."

Martha Carnes, Partner, Energy Assurance shares her favorite quote:
❝ Shoot for the moon. Even if you miss, you'll land among the stars. ❞ (Les Brown)

Although the energy industry still remains male dominated, it is changing. There are exceptional female leaders, and we need more who will change the landscape for the women who follow us. Come join us in this vibrant city and industry.

66 Decades of efforts to recruit, develop and promote women are now paying dividends to the Energy Industry. Despite the slow start and early obstacles momentum is building for women in the industry at a most important time. The baby boomer "crew change" is ongoing and it's essential to tap into the total talent pool of the nation to build the industry for the future challenges it faces. Women in Energy not only support careers, it enables the industry to fuel the 21st century. 99

—John D. Hofmeister served as a Director of U.S.A. Operations of Royal Dutch Shell. Mr. Hofmeister founded Affordable Energy Inc. and serves as its Chief Executive Officer.

Appendix:
Executive Biographies

Laura Buss Sayavedra
Vice President & CFO
Spectra Energy Partners, LP

Laura Buss is vice president and chief financial officer of Spectra Energy Partners, LP, a $3.3 billion enterprise value master limited partnership formed by Spectra Energy Corp.

Before being named to her current position in May 2008, Buss served as vice president of strategic development & analysis for Spectra Energy Corp, leading strategy, market and portfolio analysis, along with the financial evaluation of expansion projects, acquisitions and divestitures.

Buss joined the company in 1995, and has managed a broad range of assignments in the natural gas transmission, midstream gas, merchant energy and international businesses. She held positions of increasing responsibility over time, including management of international business development and acquisitions, market forecasting, operations, and strategy.

She received a Bachelor of Arts degree in international relations and economics from the University of Wisconsin-Madison in 1989, and a master's degree from Columbia University in 1991 with a focus on International Political Economy and business.

Buss is also very active in her community, serving on several non-profit Boards.

The Milwaukee native and her husband, Leo, have two sons.

Halina Caravello
Vice President, EH&S
Tyco International
(Formerly employed with Baker Hughes, Inc.)

Halina Caravello is the corporate vice president of Environmental, Health and Safety (EH&S) for Tyco International based at their headquarters in Princeton, New Jersey.

Caravello joined Tyco after 24 years at Baker Hughes, Inc. (BHI), most recently as the company's corporate vice president of HS&E, including HS&E leadership for the global Supply Chain and Products and Technology organizations.

Halina received a bachelor of science degree in biology (specialization in Marine Biology) from Fairleigh Dickinson University and a master of science degree in ecology/environmental from the University of Houston. She received her Ph.D. (2011) in leadership and organizational change from Walden University with a focus on the influence of leadership on safety performance.

She is a member of the Conference Board Chief EH&S Officers, National Association of Environmental Managers, and the Society of Petroleum Engineers and has held board positions at the Oil and Gas Producers Association, the Synthetic Organic Chemical Manufacturers Association, The Greening of Industry Network, and the Texas Association of Environmental Professionals.

Martha Z. Carnes
Partner, Energy Assurance
PricewaterhouseCoopers LLP

Martha Carnes has over twenty-eight years of experience with PricewaterhouseCoopers serving large, multi-national clients. Martha is an Assurance Partner serving clients in the energy industry, including natural gas transmission and distribution, natural gas and power trading and marketing, oil and gas exploration and production, chemicals and independent power production. Martha has held a number of leadership positions with PricewaterhouseCoopers including the Energy and Mining leader for the United States and the Houston office Market Managing Partner. She is one of the firm's global subject matter experts for the natural gas industry.

Martha is a graduate of The University of Texas at Austin where she earned a BBA degree in accounting. She is a member of the American Institute of Certified Public Accountants, the Texas and Oklahoma Societies of Certified Public Accountants, and The University of Texas Accounting Advisory Council. She is currently a member of the Board of Directors of The Greater Houston Partnership and Central Houston Inc. She is a member of the Board of Trustees for The Houston Grand Opera, serving on the Audit Committee, and The Houston Museum of Natural Science. She has previously served on the boards of The American Heart Association, Boys & Girls Clubs, and The Houston Symphony.

Cheryl Chartier
Vice President Marketing & Proposals
Foster Wheeler USA

Cheryl Chartier is the vice president of Marketing & Proposals for Foster Wheeler USA, which is a global engineering and construction contractor in the oil and gas industry. Cheryl has marketing & communications responsibilities for the company as well as commercial responsibility for all client proposals.

Cheryl has been in this industry for over 20 years. She formerly held senior positions at NATCO and KBR in Business Development, Investor Relations, Project Management and Technology Management. She has a Bachelor of Science degree in Mechanical Engineering from Carnegie Mellon University in Pennsylvania.

Cheryl's true passion is mentoring and developing talent within her organization and the industry. She speaks and trains on many topics related to sales and marketing, but is most passionate when addressing the topics of women in our industry, particularly career development and balancing demanding roles with a rewarding family life. She is an experienced speaker who routinely presents at conferences, industry forums, and other special events.

Cheryl "balances" her own life with the help of husband Larry and the understanding of her three children ages 15, 13, and 12. She is a certified fitness instructor and avid runner, and volunteers in coaching roles for children's athletics. She also serves on the Advisory Council for the Women's Energy Network. Cheryl and her family reside in Sugar Land, TX.

Janet F. Clark
Executive Vice President & Chief Financial Officer
Marathon Oil

Janet F. Clark is executive vice president and chief financial officer of Marathon Oil Corporation. Clark joined Marathon on January 5, 2004 with a strong background in financial management and energy industry experience.

She began her career as an investment banker specializing in corporate finance, primarily with The First Boston Corporation. In 1997, Clark joined Santa Fe Energy Resources, Inc. as chief financial officer. Following the merger of Santa Fe Energy and Snyder Oil in 1999, she assumed the role of executive vice president of Corporate Development and Administration. Clark joined Nuevo Energy in 2001 as senior vice president & chief financial officer.

In 1977 Clark earned a Bachelor of Arts degree in Economics from Harvard University and a Master of Business Administration degree in Finance in 1982 from the Wharton School of the University of Pennsylvania.

Clark serves on the Board of Directors of Exterran Holdings, Inc., which trades on the New York Stock Exchange under the ticker symbol EXH. She also serves on the Board of three non-profit organizations: The Houston Symphony, YES Prep Public Schools, and Greater Houston Community Foundation. Clark also serves on the Rice University-Jones Graduate School of Management Council of Overseers. Additionally, she has recently been named to the Forbes One Hundred Most Powerful Women In The World and to the Houston Woman Magazine's Houston's 50 Most Influential Women of 2010.

Cheryl R. Collarini
Energy Entrepreneur
Collarini Energy Staffing

Cheryl Collarini holds a bachelor's degree in civil engineering from M.I.T. and an MBA from the University of New Orleans. She worked for Mobil Oil as a civil engineer, operations engineer, development projects engineer, and reservoir engineering supervisor. She formed Collarini Engineering Inc. in 1985 to conduct independent reserve appraisals and field studies.

In 1995, she founded Collarini Energy Staffing to provide technical staff to customers on-site, placing upstream professionals, temporary and fulltime, in positions all over the world. In 2003, she accepted a partnership in Explore Enterprises LLC and served as VP Engineering. Explore Enterprises is an exploration and producing company with assets in the Gulf of Mexico.

In 2005, she returned to Collarini Energy Staffing after a successful sale of the Explore Enterprises assets and has since started Etroa Resources LLC, another exploration and production company located in Covington, Louisiana who desire to acquire and exploit oil and gas production in south Louisiana and to participate in the drilling of low risk oil and gas wells.

Susan M. Cunningham
Senior Vice President Exploration
Noble Energy

With over 25 years of industry experience, Susan Cunningham, who joined Noble Energy as a senior vice president in April 2001, is responsible for exploration worldwide.

Previously, she was Texaco's vice president of core worldwide exploration from April 2000 to March 2001. Employed by Statoil from 1997 through 1999, she advanced from exploration manager for deepwater Gulf of Mexico to vice president. In 1999, she assumed responsibility for Statoil's West Africa exploration efforts.

She began her career in 1980 in Calgary as a geologist at Amoco Canada, moving to Amoco's International Region in Houston in 1981 where she held various exploration and development positions until 1994, including General Manager – Denmark where she was country manager based in Copenhagen. She became exploration Manager Deepwater Gulf of Mexico in 1995 until 1997 when she joined Statoil.

Cunningham is currently Chairman of the Offshore Technology Conference representing the American Association of Petroleum Geologists (AAPG). She was elected to the Board of Cliffs Natural Resources. She also has served on the Boards of the Houston Area Women's Center and the Houston Geology Society.

Susan earned a bachelor's degree in geology and physical geography from McMaster University in Ontario, Canada. She also has completed a management program through Rice University's Office of Executive Development.

M. Cathy Douglas
Vice President, Chief Accounting Officer
Anadarko Petroleum Corporation

M. Cathy Douglas is Vice President and Chief Accounting Officer for Anadarko Petroleum Corporation, one of the world's largest independent oil and natural gas exploration and production companies. She is responsible for overseeing Anadarko's accounting functions.

Ms. Douglas joined Anadarko in 1979 as an Associate Accountant and has been Vice President and Chief Accounting Officer since November 2008. She brings to her position nearly 30 years of experience in accounting, financial reporting, internal controls and risk accounting.

Ms. Douglas has held positions of increasing responsibility throughout her career with Anadarko, including Controller, Assistant Controller, Corporate Accounting Manager and Financial Reporting Manager.

Ms. Douglas holds a Bachelor of Business Administration degree in accounting from the University of Houston. She is a member of the American Institute of Certified Public Accountants, the Texas State Board of Public Accountants and the Financial Executives Institute.

Kathleen Eisbrenner
Founder and CEO
Next Decade, LLC

Kathleen Eisbrenner is the founder and CEO for Next Decade, LLC, an entrepreneurial Liquefied Natural Gas (LNG) company committed to navigating energy frontiers. Prior to founding Next Decade in July 2010, Kathleen served as Executive Vice President Global LNG for Royal Dutch Shell in The Hague, The Netherlands. Before joining Shell in 2007, Kathleen founded Excelerate Energy in 2003 and launched a successful effort to commercialize an innovative technology and business model which proved to be very successful and continues its growth trajectory today.

Prior to Excelerate, Kathleen served as Chief Commercial Officer for El Paso Corporation, after achieving increasingly responsible roles in developing and commercializing the domestic US natural gas business.

Kathleen earned her BS in Civil Engineering from the University of Notre Dame, and further expanded her education in Marketing by participating in an Executive course at Harvard University. She has participated in non-profit and advisory boards in Houston, Texas.

Mrs. Eisbrenner is the proud mother of four children, Lynn, Michael, Ray and Michelle, and credits her husband Ray's support as the key to her success.

Lynn Laverty Elsenhans
Chief Executive Officer and President
Sunoco, Inc. and Sunoco Logistics Partners LP

Ms. Elsenhans joined Sunoco in August 2008. A veteran oil industry executive with domestic and international experience in manufacturing, marketing, and planning, Ms. Elsenhans joined Sunoco after 28 years with Royal Dutch Shell. Her last assignment with Shell was as executive vice president, global manufacturing. From 2003 to 2005, Ms. Elsenhans served concurrently as president of Shell Oil Company and president and chief executive officer of Shell Oil Products US.

Ms. Elsenhans graduated from Rice University with a Bachelor of Arts in Mathematical Science in 1978 and earned a Masters of Business Administration from Harvard Business School in 1980.

Ms. Elsenhans is on the board of directors of International Paper Company, United Way of Southeastern Pennsylvania, and the Texas Medical Center. She currently serves on the Council of Overseers for the Jones Graduate School of Business at Rice and was a member of the Rice Board of Trustees. She is married to John Elsenhans and lives in Philadelphia.

Samina Farid
Chairman and Co-Founder
Merrick Systems

Samina Farid is one of the leading energy and technology entrepreneurs in Houston. Cofounder of Merrick Systems, Farid has built the company into a global provider of industrial information technologies and professional services to the oil and gas industry.

Samina's extensive experience in the energy industry spans over four decades, and includes managerial and executive positions with ESSO Eastern, Inc., Pakistan, HNG/Enron as Director of Pipelines, Cabot Transmission and Brooklyn Interstate Natural Gas Company, a natural gas marketing company.

Since 1989, Samina has grown Merrick to be one of the largest software development companies in Houston. Merrick has been listed in the INC. 5000 since 2003, was named one of Houston Business Journal's "Fast Tech 50" companies in Houston 6 times, and one of Software Magazine's Top 500 in the nation since 2003. Other awards won by Merrick include Houston's Fastest Growing Woman Owned Businesses, Diversity.Com's Top Businesses in the US, Houston's Largest Minority Owned Businesses, Rice Alliance for Technology and Entrepreneurship's Most Promising IT Company and Most Promising Energy Company.

Samina holds a degree in business from the University of Houston. She has been involved with Houston's technology and business through the Greater Houston Partnership, Houston Technology Center and the Emerging Business Council. Samina is a member of the Board of the Houston Achievement Place which benefits Foster Children and Project CLASS.

Meg Gentle
SVP and CFO
Cheniere Energy

Meg Gentle joined Cheniere Energy, Inc. in June 2004 and was elected Senior Vice President and Chief Financial Officer of Cheniere Energy, Inc and Cheniere Energy Partners in 2009.

Prior to joining Cheniere, Meg spent eight years in energy market development, economic evaluation, and long range planning. She conducted international business development and strategic planning for Anadarko Petroleum Corporation, an oil and natural gas exploration and production company, for six years and energy market analysis for C.C. Pace Resources (now Pace Global) for two years. Meg currently serves as a director of Cheniere Energy Partners and is a member of the Governing Board of Casa de Esperanza de los Niños.

Ms. Gentle received her B.A. in Economics and International Affairs from James Madison University, and her M.B.A. from Rice University.

Paula M. Harris
Director of Community Affairs
Schlumberger

Paula Harris is a graduate of Texas A&M University with a degree in petroleum engineering. In her 25-year career in the oil industry, Harris has held a variety of positions, including field engineer managing operations on offshore rigs throughout the Gulf of Mexico. As a Field engineering Paula was often the only female, only young professional, and the only African American performing services on many of the offshore drilling rigs. It was in this position that she learned to be a manager and the skill of positively influencing others that look and think very differently than her. Other assignments included sales engineer and North American recruiting manager. As worldwide training manager, Harris developed business opportunities and teams in Europe, Africa, the Soviet Union, China, South America, and Australia. Her current assignment is director of community affairs.

Harris has received numerous recognitions, including being named to Black Engineer's "50 Who Make a Difference" and "Key Women in Energy" as well as receiving the "Women of Color in Technology". Harris has been profiled in *Black Engineer*, *Graduating Engineer*, *Money*, and *Houston Women* magazines.

Harris wrote the book *For Sister: The Guide for Professional Black Women*, published in 2003. She formed her own publishing company, Madison-House Publishing, and recently wrote and published the children's book *When I Grow UP I Want to Be an Engineer*.

Harris and her husband Dwayne are the parents of 11-year-old daughter Madison and owners of the DPM Investments.

Barbara Heim
Vice President Human Resources
BG Group, Americas & Global LNG

Barbara Heim is BG Group's Vice President Human Resources for their Americas & Global LNG region, based in Houston, TX. She is responsible for the Human Resources strategy in the region and is a member of the Regional Executive Committee and the BG Group's Human Resources Management Committee. One of her key priorities is to develop BG's talent within the region to create opportunities for individuals to grow. As a business, BG Group has been growing rapidly with establishing a large presence in Brazil, Trinidad, Bolivia and the US shale business, focusing on Louisiana and Pennsylvania shale plays.

Prior to joining BG Group, Ms. Heim spent 5 years as the VP Human Resources for Burger King in both North America and most recently, Europe, Middle East and Africa, based in Zug, Switzerland. Ms. Heim has also held HR Leadership positions in Pennzoil Quaker State, EmCare Holdings Inc., Ryder System and Colgate Palmolive. She began her adventurous career right out of college with Frito Lay Inc., spending time both in production management positions as well as Human Resources. An expert in relocation (she has moved 14 times due to her career), she has enjoyed the diversity of the industries she has worked in.

Ms. Heim serves on the advisory board of the Women's Global Leadership Conference in Energy and Technology. In addition, she serves on the advisory board for Be An Angel Fund, Inc., a non-profit benefiting children with multiple disabilities and profound deafness. This past year, Ms. Heim was the executive sponsor for BG's Habitat for Humanity build, which recently held its dedication for their fifth house.

Kathleen A. Hogenson
President & CEO
Zone Energy

With more than 27 years experience, Kathy is a leader and skilled engineer in the upstream energy industry. She is the President & CEO of Zone Energy, a Kayne Anderson backed company that she founded in 2009. Zone is an operator of oil assets in Texas and is focused on acquiring and improving US onshore based properties through technology and streamlined operations. Kathy sits on the Advisory Board for Samsung Oil & Gas.

Prior to Zone, she was President, Santos USA and Santos Americas & Europe, for six years. She rebuilt the Australian company's investment through acquisitions, exploration and drilling; and formed partnerships with several Asian companies. She sold the Americas portfolio to a private company with its base of operations in Egypt.

Kathy moved into executive leadership at Unocal Corporation. She was Vice President of Exploration & Technology and Global Chief Reservoir Engineer. Earlier, she was Engineering Manager, living in Ecuador for five years with Maxus Energy. She played a key role in driving the company's reserve value through the application of innovative technologies in a $1 billion heavy oil project.

Kathy co-founded an SPE regional office in Ecuador and serves as an SEG trustee. Kathy actively participates in YPO. She is on the Australian American Chamber of Commerce board.

She is the proud mother of two children and lucky spouse of 22 years! She holds a BS in Chemical Engineering from The Ohio State University. Kathy grew up in Grosse Pointe, Michigan.

Karyl Lawson
Head of Energy Practice
Phillips & Reiter, PLLC & Founder of Women's Energy Network

Karyl McCurdy Lawson heads the energy practice at Phillips & Reiter, PLLC. Karyl was the General Counsel of Freeport LNG LP and CMS Energy Trading and Services Company and Assistant General Counsel/Director of Government Relations in Washington, D.C. for MidCon Corp. Karyl served as a Legislative Assistant for Senator Alan Dixon (Ill.) in the Congressional Assistant Program in 1985.

Karyl founded the Women's Energy Network in 1994, www.wenhouston.org Karyl changed the way natural gas contracting was accomplished in the United States by initiating and leading the creation of the first model natural gas trading contract adopted by the predecessor of the North American Energy Standards Board.

Karyl has been committed to charitable work. She led Children at Risk's successful legislative effort that established an Independent Ombudsman for the Texas Youth Authority in the wake of sexual and physical abuse of incarcerated youth. She is a past Board member of Neighborhood Centers and Leadership Texas Alumnae Association and President of the Houston Energy Bar.

Karyl has received many awards, including one of the "50 Most Influential Women in Houston" by *Houston Woman Magazine* in 2008, the "Top 50 Women in Energy in the World" by *Commodities* Now and Accenture in 2002 and the top ten Houston businesswomen as a "Woman on the Move" from Texas Executive Women and the *Houston Chronicle*.

Gianna Manes
Senior Vice President and Chief Customer Officer
Duke Energy Corporation

As senior vice president and chief customer officer for Duke Energy, Gianna Manes is responsible for services to support Duke Energy's 4 million residential, commercial and industrial customers in North Carolina, South Carolina, Indiana, Ohio and Kentucky, including customer contacts, billing and payments, new product development and marketing, and energy efficiency initiatives. Additionally, Manes is responsible for Duke Energy's $1 billion commitment to deliver digital smart grid technology to modernize the company's power delivery system and customer interfaces.

With more than 20 years of experience in the energy industry, Manes has held leadership roles in a variety of different areas including power, gas and emissions trading; fuel procurement; power plant development, construction and operations; international and domestic gas and power business development and acquisitions; and gas pipeline operations.

Manes holds a Bachelor of Science degree in industrial engineering from Louisiana State University and an MBA from the University of Houston. She is a senior fellow with the American Leadership Forum and serves on the board of directors of Classroom Central in Charlotte, N.C.

A Louisiana native, Gianna's varied career in the energy industry has provided the opportunity to establish deep roots in Houston, Texas as well as Connecticut, Ohio, London, England and Charlotte, N.C. where she now lives with her husband and two sons.

Laurie F. Markoe
President and CEO
Contract Land Staff, LLC

Laurie Markoe is President and CEO of Contract Land Staff (CLS), LLC, a Land Management and Right of Way Consulting firm that services the energy, pipeline, utility, transportation and telecommunications industries in the U.S.

Markoe joined CLS in 1998 as the company's first marketing director. As President and COO, Markoe oversees CLS's day-to-day operations, corporate administration, operational and financial oversight, business development, client service, marketing strategy, and human resource management.

Described as forward-thinking, focused, passionate, and dynamic, Markoe has infused CLS with her own brand of energetic leadership, vision, and spirit. During her time at the helm, she has helped grow CLS into a full-fledged land and right-of-way management consulting firm with 400+ employees nationwide - all while positioning the company as a model of corporate integrity.

Markoe is an active member of the International Right of Way Association's International Pipeline Committee, the American Association of Professional Landmen, serving as President of the IRWA's Houston chapter. She serves on the IRWA's International Communications and Marketing Committee and she serves as Vice Chair for the Interstate Natural Gas Association of America (INGAA) Executive Committee and Board of Directors. Laurie is a former board member of the Women's Energy Network of Houston and South Texas Girl Scout Council, and she is a lifelong Girl Scout volunteer.

Rebecca McDonald
Chief Executive Officer
Laurus Energy, Inc.

Rebecca McDonald was named as the chief executive officer of Laurus Energy, Inc. in 2008.

Prior to her appointment at Laurus, Rebecca served as president gas and power for BHP Billiton and was responsible for the worldwide natural gas marketing and commercialization strategy.

With over 25 years of experience in the energy industry, she has held a multitude of strategic positions including president of the Houston Museum of Natural Science and independent director of BOC Group in the U.K., Trammell Crow Corporation, Eagle Global Logistics, Morton International and Noble Energy.

Rebecca currently serves as the independent presiding director for Granite Construction Company and is an independent director of Veresen, Inc., a Canadian Gas and Power Infrastructure Corporation, headquarter in Calgary, Canada. She serves on the boards of the Chinquapin School Advisory Board, Inprint, the Women's Initiative of the United Way Steering Committee and Graduate School of Business for SFASU. She holds a BS from Stephen F. Austin State University.

Melody B. Meyer
President
Chevron Asia Pacific Exploration and Production Company

Melody Meyer is President of Chevron Asia Pacific Exploration and Production Company, a position she assumed in March 2011..

Prior to assuming this position, Meyer was President of Chevron's Energy Technology Company, where she was responsible for the company's global upstream and downstream technology research and development and technical services to Chevron operating companies worldwide.

Meyer has spent 19 of her 31 years at Chevron working on international projects, 10 years in key leadership roles in North America Exploration and Production, and 3 years leading technology. She was Vice President of Chevron's Gulf of Mexico strategic business unit responsible for offshore exploration and production operations in the Gulf of Mexico, and has served as Vice President of the MidContinent/Alaska business unit.

Meyer graduated from Trinity University in 1979 with a bachelor's degree in Engineering Science-Mechanical. She attended Dartmouth Tuck Executive Education program in 1997.

Meyer is the Executive Sponsor of the Chevron Women's Network and for the University Partnership Program with the University of Texas at Austin. She is on the Executive Committee and Board of the National Ocean Industry Association, and Board of Trustees of Trinity University. In 2009, Meyer was honored as Trinity University Distinguished Alumni; by BioHouston with an award honoring Women in Science; and by the American Society of Mechanical Engineers as the Rhoades Petroleum Industry Leadership Award recipient.

Peggy Montana
Executive Vice President Supply & Distribution
Shell Downstream, Inc.

Peggy Montana is executive vice president of supply & distribution at Shell Downstream, Inc. She is responsible for hydrocarbon supply to Shell's manufacturing and marketing businesses worldwide.

Peggy's career with Shell began in 1977 at the Deer Park Refinery, followed by positions of increasing responsibility in refining and chemical sites, research and development, and the head office. In 1995 she joined Shell's lubricants business and rose to lead the US lubricants supply chain. In 2001, Peggy became general manager of distribution for Shell's Asia Pacific business based in Singapore. She returned to the US in 2004 as vice president of supply and then was named vice president of global distribution where she led Shell's fuels terminaling and distribution activities worldwide. She assumed her present responsibilities in 2009.

Peggy holds a Bachelor of Chemical Engineering degree from Missouri Science & Technology University. She serves on the boards of the Houston Area Urban League and the YMCA. She is married with two children and resides in Houston Texas.

Suzanne Paquin Nimocks
Independent Director
Encana

Suzanne is a member of the Board of Directors for EnCana, a natural gas exploration and production company based in Calgary, Canada.

Suzanne is a recently retired Director (senior partner) in McKinsey & Company's Houston Office. Since joining the Firm in 1989, she served clients in energy, logistics, manufacturing, and professional services industries on a broad range of strategy, corporate finance, business building, portfolio management, operations, organization, and risk management-related issues.

In addition to client work, Suzanne was a leader in the Firm's Global Petroleum Practice, Electric Power & Natural Gas Practice, as well as the Global Organization Practice.

Prior to joining McKinsey, Suzanne spent two years with the New York and London Offices of Strategic Planning Associates. In addition, she spent four years as an Account Executive with Travelers.

Suzanne sits on the Executive Committee of the Greater Houston Partnership and chairs the Environmental Policy Committee. She is a Trustee for the St. John's School in Houston. She is a former board member of the United Way of the Texas Gulf Coast, the Houston Zoo, and the American Heart Association.

Suzanne holds a Bachelor of Arts degree in Economics from Tufts University and a Masters in Business Administration from the Harvard Graduate School of Business. She is married and the mother of a 21 year old son and 19 year old daughter.

Sue Ortenstone
Executive Vice President and Chief Administrative Officer
El Paso Corporation

Sue Ortenstone is executive vice president and chief administrative officer for El Paso Corporation. In her current role, Ortenstone oversees Human Resources, Communications and Community Relations, IT, Facilities and Real Estate functions for the company. A major focus for her is driving the company's culture transformation across the organization. The new performance driven culture focuses on talent management, leadership development, recognition and the employee experience and achieving the company's vision of being the Place to Work, the Neighbor to Have and the Company to Own.

Ortenstone began her career as an engineer in training for Tennessee Gas Pipeline, a division of Tenneco, Inc. She has held various positions with increasing levels of responsibility in engineering, operations, marketing, business development and strategy. Her most recent previous position was chief executive officer of Epic Energy, Australia's largest natural gas pipeline company at that time.

Ortenstone earned a Bachelor of Science degree in civil and environmental engineering from the University of Wisconsin and is a registered professional engineer. She is on the Board of Junior Achievement, the Houston Area Women's Center, the Advisory Board for the University of Texas College of Engineering and the Business Advisory Council for Goodwill Industries.

Sharon M. Owens
Vice President of Corporate Community
Centerpoint Energy

Sharon M. Owens, Vice President of Centerpoint Energy's Corporate Community Relations Department, oversees the strategic development and implementation of the company's community based programs specializing in Education and Consumer Affairs and corporate giving. In addition to managing and developing her staff in Houston and Minnesota, she works closely with the Executive leadership to provide strategic direction as it relates to the community and CenterPoint energy's core business.

Owens is active on several professional and civic boards and is currently president of the Missouri City Chapter of Links. She has received numerous awards and recognition for her leadership and invaluable services to the community, in which she works and lives.

She considers herself both a catalyst and conduit for people to achieve positive goals for themselves and their community. She has the ability and intuition to assess needs in the community and match the right people with the right causes to achieve the right results.

Owens received her A.A Degree from St. Philip's Jr. College in San Antonio, Texas, and her B.S. in Vocational Education from Tennessee State University in Nashville, Tennessee. She taught high school in St Paul, Minnesota prior to joining CenterPoint Energy (HL&P) in 1977.

Annise D. Parker
Mayor, City of Houston

Mayor Annise Parker is a second generation native Houstonian. She attended Rice University, graduating with a Bachelor of Arts Degree. In the private sector, Ms. Parker spent 20 years working in the oil and gas industry, including 18 years with Mosbacher Energy Company. She also co-owned a retail bookstore for 10 years.

Mayor Parker was sworn in to her first term as mayor of Houston on January 4, 2010. She is Houston's 61st Mayor, one of only two women to hold the City's highest elected office. As the City's chief executive officer she is responsible for all aspects of the general management of the City and for seeing that all laws and ordinances are enforced.

Prior to her election as Mayor, Ms. Parker served for six years as Houston City Controller and six years as an at-large member of Houston City Council. She is the only person in Houston history to hold the offices of council member, controller and mayor.

Sue Payne
Chief Operating Officer
National Math and Science Initiative Representing ExxonMobil

Sue Payne joined the National Math and Science Initiative as Chief Operating Officer in 2011 from ExxonMobil Corporation.

A native of Hickory Flat, Georgia, Ms. Payne graduated from Georgia Institute of Technology with a Bachelor of Science degree in Physics.

Ms. Payne joined Mobil in 1976 as a geoscientist in Dallas, Texas. During her 35 years with Mobil, and now ExxonMobil, her management and operations experiences have afforded her a variety of assignments. She has been Planning Manager for ExxonMobil Exploration Company; U.S. Area Exploration Manager; Geoscience Operations Manager for ExxonMobil Production Company; Vice President for Mobil's Onshore U.S. Producing Business; Commercial and Negotiations Manager for Mobil New Business Development in Latin America; and an advisor at Mobil's corporate headquarters. Ms. Payne has held positions in Lagos, Nigeria; New Orleans, Louisiana; Fairfax, Virginia; Dallas and Houston, Texas.

Before assuming her current position at NMSI, her role as Geoscience Resource Manager encompassed managing the training, career development, and project deployment for more than 1,500 geoscientists in ExxonMobil's worldwide operations.

A member of numerous charitable and civic organizations, Ms. Payne has recently completed her second term as Co-Chairman of the United Way of Greater Houston Women's Initiative and is an active member of the Georgia Tech Alumni Association. She also was recently named one of "Houston's 50 Most Influential Women" by Houston Women's Magazine.

Charlene A. Ripley
SVP, General Counsel and Corporate Secretary
LINN Energy

Charlene A. Ripley is LINN Energy's Senior Vice President, General Counsel and Corporate Secretary. She oversees the company's legal, information technology, corporate governance and compliance, government affairs, and insurance and risk-management departments. She has extensive domestic and international experience.

Ms. Ripley holds a Bachelor of Arts, with distinction, from the University of Alberta. She earned her law degree from Dalhousie University in Halifax, Nova Scotia. She currently chairs the Oil and Gas Practice Committee of the Institute for Energy Law and serves on the board of the Texas General Counsel Forum. She is also the past President of The Woodlands Bar Association, which she helped found.

Ms. Ripley serves on the advisory boards of the Women's Energy Network and Executive Women's Partnership of the Greater Houston Partnership. She serves on several non-profit boards including the Youth Development Center, Girls Inc. and the American Heart Association of Houston. She is a member of the United Way of Greater Houston Women's Initiative.

Ms. Ripley received the 2010 Magna Stella Award from the Texas General Counsel Forum for in-house excellence in leadership and management. She was the recipient of the Houston Business Journal's Best Corporate Counsel Award in 2009 for "Best Corporate Counsel with a Staff of two to 10" and in 2006 for "Best Handling of a Complex, Difficult or Challenging Issue."

Maryann T. Seaman
Vice President, Treasurer and Deputy Chief Financial Officer
FMC Technologies

Maryann T. Seaman is Vice President, Treasurer and Deputy Chief Financial Officer for FMC Technologies.

Ms. Seaman was appointed Vice President, Treasurer and Deputy Chief Financial Officer in April 2010. She held the position of Vice President of Administration from 2007 through 2010 and was responsible for Human Resources, Executive Compensation, Health, Safety and Environment and Corporate Communications. She also served as the Secretary to the Compensation and the Nominating and Governance Committees of the Board of Directors.

In 2005, Ms. Seaman became responsible for Corporate Communications in addition to holding the position of Director of Investor Relations and Corporate Development, which she held since 2003. Previously, she served as Group Controller of FoodTech since 2000 as well as Division Controller of the Airport Systems Division in 1996. In 1993, Ms. Seaman became the Finance and Operations Manager for the North American Division of the Agricultural Products Group of FMC Corporation, located in Philadelphia. Prior to this, she was the Facilities Administration Manager for the Agricultural Products Group's Research and Development Center.

Before joining FMC Corporation in 1986, Ms. Seaman served as Finance Manager for Sheller-Globe Corporation.

She holds a Bachelor's Degree in Accounting and an MBA from Rider University in Lawrenceville, New Jersey.

Cindy B. Taylor
President, Chief Executive Officer and Director
Oil States International, Inc.

Cindy B. Taylor is the President, Chief Executive Officer and Director of Oil States International, Inc., a diversified oilfield services company that trades on the NYSE. Prior to assuming this position, Ms. Taylor served as President and Chief Operating Officer from May 2006 to April 2007 and as Oil States' Senior Vice President — Chief Financial Officer and Treasurer from May 2000 to April 2006. Prior to joining Oil States, Ms. Taylor served as the Chief Financial Officer of L.E. Simmons & Associates, Incorporated (SCF Partners), a private equity firm specializing in oilfield service investments. It was during her tenure at SCF Partners that she helped lead the effort to merge four private companies and take them public via an Initial Public Offering in 2001 which then became Oil States International, Inc. She also served as the Vice President – Controller of Cliffs Drilling Company, a contract drilling company, from July 1992 to August 1999 and worked in public accounting from January 1984 to July 1992. During her entire public accounting career, she served companies in the energy industry.

Ms. Taylor is currently a director of Tidewater Inc., a global vessel operator servicing the oil and gas industry. She received a B.B.A. degree from Texas A&M University and is a Certified Public Accountant. She is active in many industry and community organizations and is married with three children.

Jamie L. Vazquez
President
W&T Offshore

Jamie L. Vasquez was appointed President of W&T Offshore in September 2008.

Ms. Vazquez joined the Company in 1998 and was most recently Vice President, Land, a position she has held since 2003.

Prior to joining W&T Offshore, Ms. Vazquez was with CNG Producing Company for 17 years lastly serving as Manager, Land/Business Development Gulf of Mexico with prior experience as Onshore Land Manager and Senior Landman-Mid-Continent Region.

She is on the advisory council for Women's Energy Network.

Ms. Vazquez received a B.S. in Management from University of Tulsa in 1984. She is married with children.

Martha B. Wyrsch
President
Vestas-American Wind Technology, Inc.

Martha B. Wyrsch is President of Vestas-American Wind Technology, Inc., the North American arm of Vestas Wind Systems, the world's largest manufacturer of wind turbines. Wyrsch joined Vestas in June 2009.

She serves on the Executive Committee for Vestas Wind Systems A/S, based in Randers, Denmark, the parent company for Vestas' North American operations. Wyrsch is a member of the National Infrastructure Advisory Council, a White House advisory board through the U.S. Secretary of Homeland Security, and the National Petroleum Council, a White House Advisory Board through the U.S. Secretary of Energy. She is a member of the Board of Directors and Leadership Council of the American Wind Energy Association (AWEA) and serves on the Board of Directors of SPX Corporation, a Fortune 500 company based in Charlotte, North Carolina.

Prior to Vestas, Wyrsch was CEO for Spectra Energy Transmission and a member of the Spectra Energy Board of Directors. Prior to that, she was CEO of Duke Energy Gas Transmission. In both roles, she was responsible for the natural gas transmission, storage and distribution businesses in the United States and Canada, as well as natural-gas gathering, processing and liquid sales businesses in Canada. Wyrsch also served as Group Vice President, General Counsel and Secretary for the Duke Energy Corporation.

A native of Laramie, Wyoming, Wyrsch earned a law degree from George Washington University and bachelor's degree from the University of Wyoming. She also completed the Harvard Business School Advanced Management Program.

Joan Eischen
Author
"Energy and the City"
Director, Advisory
KPMG LLC Houston

Joan Eischen is a Director for advisory services with KPMG LLP, the U.S. audit, tax and advisory services firm.

She is an International Business Development Specialist with more than 20 years' experience working in complex product and services sales in Europe, Latin America and North America. Prior to joining KPMG, she was the Client Manager at Logica Inc., the North American headquarters of a global services company, leading the development of their Health, Safety and Environment practice.

She was vice president of sales in Latin America for Rite Hite, an American manufacturer of safety and warehouse logistics capital equipment. She established a distribution chain throughout Latin America that still thrives today. It was in this role, that Eischen was an expat for her company.

Eischen served three years as program director for the Women's Energy Network. She is on the advisory board for Houston Achievement Place (www.hapkids.org), a social service agency that helps children, youth and families.

She earned a B.B.A. in International Business from the University of Wisconsin and specialized in Strategic Sales Management at the University of Chicago. She is fluent in Spanish, proficient in Portuguese, and active in IADC and SPE.

Barbara S. Lavery, Ph.D.
Independent Consultant

Barbara S. Lavery runs an independent consulting practice in which she serves clients as an organizational consultant and executive coach. She has coached in numerous Fortune 500 companies and specializes in working with individuals who are in emerging leadership positions or are in major change agent roles.

Prior to developing her independent practice, she worked for Personnel Decisions International as an Executive Consultant and as Director of World Wide Coaching Services. During that time she was responsible for delivering executive coaching services across North America as well as supporting team members in building the company's global coaching capabilities.

Before joining PDI she worked for over 25 years in a number of private and non-profit mental health settings both as a direct service provider and in mental health management. As the Clinical Director of a Houston area community mental health agency for over eight years, she was responsible for the development, training and ongoing coaching of professional staff and interns. In addition, she was active in community education initiatives, grant writing, program development and program evaluation.

Ms. Lavery has served on a number of advisory community boards including Youth & Family Counseling Services of Brazoria County and as Chair of the Mental Health Community Management Team of Galveston and Brazoria Counties.

Barbara received a bachelor's degree from Illinois Wesleyan University, has a master's degree in Clinical Psychology from Eastern Illinois University and a Ph.D. in Developmental Psychology from the University of Houston.

Cecilia Rose
ICF Credentialed Coach

Cecilia Rose is an ICF Credentialed Coach, with 15 years as a trusted advisor, and career and change management strategist working with global Fortune 50 and 500 companies. Cecilia's passion is partnering with senior executives to achieve their personal and business goals while enhancing their leadership skills. She leads and facilitates executive roundtables and has made presentations on How to Navigate Corporate Change, Sales and Marketing Strategies, Career Management, Leadership Development and Emotional & Relationship intelligence.

Cecilia has over 25 years of business experience in sales & marketing, career development, training, and retail operations. Her style is people–centric with the unique combination of business acumen, intuition, analytical skills and career expertise that spans a wide range of functions, disciplines and industries.

She is a compelling keynote speaker and trainer, skilled in presenting workshops including, "Managing Your Career", "Career Transition in the 21st Century", "Executive Straight Talk", and "On the Road to Entrepreneurialism". She created "The NEXT DOOR Workshop" for executives asking the question, "What's next?".

She taught and has co-written for the University of Houston Small Business Development Center. She has been interviewed and quoted by Forbes Magazine, Kiplinger's Personal Finance Magazine, 20/20 and ExecuNET.

Cecilia is a MCC Master Coach Candidate and ACC Credentialed Executive and Career Coach with the International Coach Federation. She is a graduate of Coach University and has a Bachelor of Science Degree from the University of Spirituality and Health.